Sunset Painting
&
The Sun

Two Plays
by Greg Klein

The Sun … Copyright 2023
Sunset Painting … Copyright 2023

ISBN: 978-1-7378635-1-9

Dedicated to Ludmilla Selihova Evans, aka Lala la petite ballerine, my grandmother, the child star, and the light and dark of our lives.

Sunset Painting

Cast Breakdown

Gregory: Male, mid-20s, a want-to-be wrestler turned actor who moves in with his dying grandmother.
Lala: Female, 80s, of Russian descent who used to be a child star as a ballerina, but whose life changed when her husband died young of a rare disease.
Jenny: Female, 50s, Lala's younger daughter, Gregory's mom, a lawyer who came of age in the 1960s and struggles with her addictions.
Lynn: Female, 60s, Lala's older daughter, more of a child of the 1950s, fled home for early entry to college after her father died.
Lawrence: Male, 50s, African-American, Jenny's boyfriend.
Debbie: Female, 40s, African-American woman who becomes La3la's nurse.

Act ONE, Scene ONE

A large, rundown house overlooking the Hudson River in Westchester County, New York, in the late 1990s. Pet fur, dust, old magazines and ash are all around. On the first floor is a kitchen on one end, a living room on the other. Both have doorways to other rooms. On the second floor are two bedrooms and more. The downstairs area is filled with ashtrays, an old couch, an old TV.

LALA, 80s, is an old Russian woman. Her accent has been dulled by 60 years of living in New York, but is still there. She is petite, and despite her age, still has the poise of a dancer. Next to her couch is a small, round table. On it are a TV remote, a newspaper, magazines, glasses, an ashtray, cigarettes, a bottle of vodka and a shot glass.

GREGORY, 26, is about 5-11, well built.

JENNY, 50s, is overweight, redheaded. She's a woman who came of age in the 60s and did too much of everything.

JENNY
Hello. Is anyone home? Mother?

LALA
Hello? Jenny? Is that you?

JENNY
Not just me. But also …

He has a big box in the arms.

GREGORY
Hi, Ga.

LALA
Oh Gregory! I am glad to see you. Put that down. Sit down.

GREGORY
There's a lot more in the truck.

LALA
Do it later. I'm so glad to see you. You've gotten big.

JENNY
He's a big guy now. A real grown-up.

GREGORY
I hope it's okay. Me moving in with you.

LALA
Of course it is. I never got why you stayed in Alabama.

GREGORY
Well, it's where I got a job. Where all my journalism professors had their contacts.

LALA
Yes, but it was so far away.

JENNY
Well, it doesn't matter now. He's here.

GREGORY
I'm going to go get more stuff out of the truck.

He exits.

LALA
Oh, Jenny. I worry about you. I didn't used to worry so much. But since the divorce.

JENNY
I know, mother.

LALA
I'm happy to have Gregory here.

JENNY
Yes. He's happy to be here.

LALA
I don't think he was really happy in Alabama.

JENNY
No, I guess not.

LALA
Are you happy?

JENNY
Yes, mother.

LALA
How is Steve?

JENNY
He's fine, mother.

LALA
I always liked him.

JENNY
I did, too, right up to the point where he was cheating on me. Or me on him. Anyway. We've talked about this, mother Can we talk about something else?

LALA
I worry about Lynn, but not the same. She's always capable.

JENNY
You know, mom, I am a lawyer.

LALA
I know. That's not what I mean. She left home at 16, right after your father died. You were here much longer.

JENNY
Not much longer, mom. I left at 18.

LALA
But that was eight more years with me. And then you went to school in the city.

JENNY
I'm going to help Gregory.

LALA
I wish I could help, too.

JENNY
You are helping.

LALA
Well, he'll be a big help to me. I don't want to be a burden.

JENNY
I know. I'm going to help with the unpacking.

She leaves. GREGORY enters with a box.

LALA
Are you leaving again?

GREGORY
No, I'm just unpacking.

LALA
I mean later. Your mom said something about Florida.

GREGORY
Yes. I have matches I am booked for in Florida. I'll drive down, wrestle, maybe see some friends and drive back up.

LALA
To here? For good?

GREGORY
Yes.

LALA
What about your cats?

GREGORY
They'll be fine. Just put some food out for them. Some water. They'll probably hide for a while.

LALA
Oh, are they 'fraidy cats?

GREGORY
It's just, they didn't have a lot of people around them in Alabama. Just me, mostly.

LALA
I wish you didn't have to go back so soon.

GREGORY
I know. But I'll be back for good in two weeks. I'm going to go finish unpacking before Mom thinks I left it to her.

He leaves. LALA walks upstairs with cat food. A half dozen bowls are out.

LALA
Mystery. Hoobie. Strange name for a cat if you ask me. Gregory will never forgive me if I've lost his cats. Why did he have to leave for so long? Has it been so long? It's hard to keep track of the days. I have a calendar, it's just that I don't have reason to use it.

Mystery, is that you? Well, it looks like someone has been eating the food I left yesterday. Or was that the day before? Did I bring all these bowls up?

GREGORY

I was staying with a friend and his wife in Florida. Before I arrived, my grandmother had called a dozen times. When I got there and called her to make sure everything was alright, she cried and told me she had lost my cats. I called my mom, and she said she was going to go back up to New York, and I should get home as soon as possible.

LALA

Hello? Lynn?

JENNY

No, mother it's me.

LALA

Oh, Jenny. I didn't recognize you. I thought maybe Gregory was back home.

JENNY

Not yet.

LALA

You look different.

JENNY

I know, mother. I've put on weight.

LALA
You've put on weight.

She goes upstairs. LALA follows. JENNY starts to pick up the old bowls.

JENNY
I just said that. Oh, mother. That's a lot of food bowls.

LALA
I was afraid they would starve.

JENNY
Clearly they've been eating food.

LALA
They didn't eat all of it.

JENNY
That might be because there is so much of it.

She looks under the bed, in the closet.

JENNY
Hello, girls. Don't be scared. They're in the closet.

LALA
Oh. And I looked there. Several times. Fresh cats.

Downstairs, GREGORY enters.

GREGORY
Hello? Anyone here?

JENNY and LALA come down the stairs.

JENNY
Hi, I am so glad you are home. You don't know how stressful this was. I had to make a special trip back up here.

LALA
Oh, Gregory. I was so worried.

GREGORY
You don't have to worry.

LALA
But what if I had lost your cats? Would you have forgiven me?

GREGORY
Yes, I would have. But the important thing is they're safe, and I'm here, and I don't have anywhere to go for weeks.

JENNY
And I have to get home.

LALA
Oh, Jenny, can't you stay longer?

JENNY
No. I left work to come here. I've got a lot to do back home.

LALA
Oh, my Jenny. Always leaving.

JENNY
To work, Mom. And I always come back.

LALA
When?

JENNY
A couple of months, maybe. I will definitely come for Easter.

LALA
When is that?

JENNY
April.

LALA
And this is?

JENNY
January.

LALA
February, March, April. Three whole months?

JENNY
It won't be that long. And now you've got Gregory here.

LALA
That's true. At least I have good company.

JENNY goes downstage. LALA goes to her couch, pours a shot, has a sip. GREGORY goes up to his room, unpacks.

JENNY
My father died when I was 10.

LALA
My father was thrown in prison when I was eight.

GREGORY
My father was thrown out of the house when I was four.

ALL
I didn't know how to deal with it.

JENNY
My sister, she was his favorite. She was 16, and she got into Dartmouth. We expected her to stay home. She told us no way.

LALA
He was an officer in the White Army, and the Bolsheviks caught him and put him into prison.

GREGORY
He's a doctor. What girl doesn't want to be a doctor's wife? My mom, apparently. She told him ...

JENNY
I wasn't in love with him anymore.

GREGORY
I didn't know you could fall out of love with someone. I think all my young life, I worried girlfriends would fall out of love with me. And they did. Just like I feared.

LALA
I don't know about this love thing, really.

JENNY
Sometimes I think love is overrated.

GREGORY
My last girlfriend broke up with me because I wanted to spend my weekends wrestling. She said, "I just don't think you can do the things in life you want to do." And then, she took up with another guy. Immediately. That was a few years ago.

LALA

I mean, you love someone, and then they are gone.

JENNY

I ended up cheating on both of my husbands. So that's my fault, I guess. Although, as it turns out, my second husband was cheating on me long before I was cheating on him.

LALA

I grew up in a different era, I guess. It's not that people didn't have affairs. But not Irving and me. I was dancing at Radio City, in the ballet troop. He oversaw us, 100 or more girls. Ballerinas. Rockettes. Long-legged girls. Big-breasted girls. Beautiful girls. And it was me he asked out. I didn't think he could be interested in me. Out of all those girls.

JENNY

I was 10 when my father died. It wasn't fair.

LALA

He was only 44. Who dies from arthritis? And in their 40s?

GREGORY

What made it such a tragedy, I think, is it never stopped being a tragedy in their eyes.

LALA
Everyone said "you should sell the house, it's too big for you now. The girls will move out, and then you'll be all alone." I was already all alone. If I sold the house, I would still be all alone. I just wouldn't have a home.

JENNY
What I don't remember is him. Who he was. As a person. I hear the stories. All the same stories, over and over again.

LALA
Did I tell you about when Irving was working at the Music Hall? (Beat) One time, he was hosting a World War II benefit for that fellow from the late night show. You know the one?

GREGORY
The Tonight Show?

LALA
No, the other one. Oh, what was his name? Ed Sullivan!

GREGORY
My grandfather hosted a benefit for Ed Sullivan?

LALA
We have a letter thanking him somewhere. Your father that is.

GREGORY
You mean Irving?

LALA
Yes, he was worried about it. Sullivan, that is. He was always calling. Irving knew what a big thing it was. He'd come home at 11 p.m., and I'd make him some eggs. He liked eggs at night, your father. *(She lights a cigarette, offers him one.)* You can if you like. I know you have a smoke now and again. You don't have to hide it. You're a grown man now. Anyway, where was I?

GREGORY
Ed Sullivan.

LALA
Every night I'd ask Irving how it was going, and he'd say, "honey, our boys are over there fighting for our country. All I'm doing is throwing a great party in their honor." And he did. Every letter Ed Sullivan sent ended, "please tell your lovely wife hello for me." What was my point anyway?

GREGORY
I don't know. But it was a great story.

LALA
I'm sorry you didn't meet him. He'd like you. I don't know what he'd make of this wrestling though. It's so barbaric.

GREGORY
I don't know. I guess I like it.

LALA
I don't mind if you come and go. I keep odd hours myself. When you get to be my age, what difference does day and night make? I'll worry if you're later than one or two. Midnight, I don't worry. The witching hour. Like all good witches.

GREGORY
Right. That's me. A good witch.

LALA
I'm glad you're here, Gregory.

GREGORY
Yeah, I'm glad I'm here, too.

Act ONE, Scene TWO

Months later. GREGORY and LALA are cleaning. LALA picks pet hair off the carpet. GREGORY stacks clutter.

LALA
Gregory. GREGORY!

GREGORY
I'm right here, honey.

LALA
Oh, there you are. I thought you were upstairs.

GREGORY
Did you need something?

LALA
I don't know. I just wanted to make sure we had some things for Lynn to, you know, nosh on.

GREGORY
We do.

LALA
We do?

GREGORY
Yes. I went shopping earlier in the day.

LALA
You did? Do I remember that?

GREGORY
I'm not sure, honey, but I got lunch meats, some cokes and juice, some cheese, and lots of the pastries you guys like.

LALA
Oooh, that sounds good.

GREGORY
Didn't I see you eating a cheese Danish earlier?

LALA
Did you? I don't remember.

GREGORY
Yes, I think I did. Well, there's more if you want it.

They move to the kitchen. LALA gets a Danish. GREGORY pours soda.

LALA
That's good. Will you plug in that water and hand me the instant coffee? I wanted to ask you about something. You know about the bracelet my friend Irina sent us?

GREGORY
Yes. I have heard about it.

LALA
Well, Irina sent it to me. And last time Lynn was here she took it and said she was going to have it appraised and send it back to me. But she never sent it back to me.

GREGORY
What did she say?

LALA
She didn't want to send it. It makes me so angry. I didn't raise a thief. Irving and I did not raise a thief.

GREGORY
I'm sure she thinks she's entitled. It is to be her's, right?

LALA
But don't whisk it away. I barely got a chance to see it.

GREGORY
I don't know how to tell you this, but I don't think she'll ever bring that bracelet back.

LALA
My own daughter. Irving's daughter. It makes me so angry. How could she do that to me?

GREGORY
I don't think she was doing that to you. She was doing something she felt was right.

LALA
The thing is, it makes me so angry.

GREGORY
Okay, honey, I know that. You're just going round in circles, and I have to go to work in a little while.

LALA
Oh. I forgot.

GREGORY
It's why I got up early and got groceries.

LALA
Oh Gregory, but what about ciggies?

He pulls a carton off the shelf and waves it. She takes it with gusto. He begins to pack a lunch.

LALA
Oh, Gregory, I love you.

GREGORY
I love you, too. I would have gotten your vodka, too, but they weren't open yet.

LALA
I called the liquor store. He said he didn't have anyone yesterday, but he has someone coming in today.

GREGORY
I don't want to be late. We have a school group coming in.

LALA
Where are you working again?

GREGORY
Sunnyside.

LALA
Sunnyside. I feel like I know that.

GREGORY
It's the museum down the street.

LALA
Oh yes. Is that the same place you work at night?

GREGORY
Sometimes. Sometimes I am at Philipsburg.

LALA
Philipsburg. I meant to ask, are there people there with you?

GREGORY
When I give tours. Yes.

LALA
No, I mean at night. Sometimes you work so late.

GREGORY
No. Not at night. At night I am guarding, keeping people out.

LALA
Oh. So just you and the ghosts? (beat) Oh, Gregory. I always look forward to Lynn coming, but I am so angry at her.

GREGORY
I know. Try to talk to her about it. I have to go.

LALA
When will you be home?

GREGORY
For good at one, maybe for a half hour or so in between shifts if I get a break.

LALA
I don't know, is there any food for Lynn?

GREGORY
Yes, I told you, I went shopping this morning. You've got a bun right there next to you.

LALA
So I do. You don't have to rub it in.

GREGORY
Sorry. Your water's ready. Give me your mug. Besides Lynn will just go to the store after she gets here anyway.

LALA
How do you know?

GREGORY
That's what she does. Alright. Have a good day. I love you.

He kisses her.

LALA
I love you, too. Be safe. Oh, and do I have cigarettes?

Act ONE, Scene THREE

LALA reads a paper in the kitchen. LYNN, 60s, enters. She is heavy set, but professional looking. She carries cigarettes and a huge mug of coffee.

LYNN
Hello? Anyone home? Mother?

LALA
Oh, Lynn, I'm in here.

LYNN
Hello. You're looking well.

LALA
I do not, and you know it. But you look well. Are you hungry?

LYNN
No, I ate at the airport, and I have groceries in the car. I'll get them in a minute, but I want to have a cigarette.

LALA
I think Gregory went shopping today.

LYNN
That's fine. I need stuff for dinner. And for the pashka.

LALA
Oh, Lynn, I was hoping you would make pashka.

LYNN
And tonight I am going to make meat and eggplant pies.

LALA
That's wonderful, but you don't have to. You work so hard.

LYNN
Yes, I do. But this is different. This is cooking. I enjoy it, especially for you. You need some meat on your bones.

LALA
How long are you staying?

LYNN
Long enough to make pashka, and not much longer than that. I have to fly out and then work Monday.

LALA
You're so busy all the time. I worry.

LYNN
I worry about you, too. Where's Gregory?

LALA
He's at work.

LYNN
He's working? That's good.

LALA
Yes. I can't remember where. Some museum. Funnyside.

LYNN
I'll be right back. I'm going to get some stuff out of the car. I'll leave my suitcase for Gregory when he gets home.

LALA
I wanted to ask you something.

LYNN
I'll be back in a minute.

LALA
Funnyside. Fuddyside. Sillyside. Sunnyside. Sunnyside? Yes, Sunnyside. That must be it. Now where are my cigarettes?

LYNN returns with groceries.

LYNN
Oh mother. Is Gregory buying you vodka now?

LALA
No! Well, maybe if I ask. But they deliver to me.

LYNN
I've asked them not to do that.

LALA
Listen, I am a grown woman, and if I have a sip of vodka now and then, I don't see what's wrong with that. Besides I had a doctor tell me it was good for me to have a drink.

LYNN
That was in the 1950s, just after father's death, and he said a drink, as in one drink a day.

LALA
Well, this is my first drink today! They just delivered the bottle not long ago.

LYNN

It seems like more than one shot is already gone from it.

LALA

Maybe it is my second. My memory isn't what it used to be. You know, Lynn, I wanted to ask you about Irina's bracelet.

LYNN

Again, Mother?

LALA

I don't remember talking about it with you before.

LYNN

We talked about it when I took the bracelet, and we have talked about it every time we've talked since then.

LALA

Well, what did you tell me?

LYNN

I took it for safe keeping.

LALA

Why isn't it safe here?

LYNN

How many times have you had stuff stolen from here?

LALA

Not very often.

LYNN

You tell me all the time the tenants are stealing from you.

LALA

Well, that one, Beverly, yes.

LYNN

More than one. Just one recently. Jenny and I bought you a VCR for Christmas a few years ago. Do you know where it is?

LALA

I'm not even sure I know what it is.

LYNN

A VCR. You play movies on it.

LALA

Really? I would like something like that.

LYNN

You had that tenant about 10 years ago whose boyfriend stole all of your jewelry. Remember?

LALA

Yes. That I remember.

LYNN
So why would I leave a thousand-dollar bracelet lying around your house? Especially when it was meant as a present for me.

LALA
You don't just take things.

LYNN
That's my point exactly. But some people do.

LALA
Yes, but I just didn't think it would be my own daughter.

LYNN
Mother. I'm not having this argument with you.

LALA
I want you to bring the bracelet back.

LYNN
It's in a safety deposit box. That's all I'm going to say.

LALA
You can't just end the conversation that way.

LYNN
I am. I have to go get my suitcase.

LALA
Gregory can get it.

LYNN
I'm going to get something out of the car.

LALA
Lynn get back here and talk to me.

LYNN
No, mother, I'm not a child. You've made your point.

She leaves. LALA finds her shot glass, takes a drink. Pours another. LYNN reenters.

LYNN
There's another thing, mother.

LALA
Can we just discuss one thing at a time?

LYNN
We've dealt with the other thing. My turn now.

LALA
We haven't finished.

LYNN
What else could you possibly have to say?

LALA
Irving and I didn't raise you ...
LYNN
Fine, you didn't.

LALA
You didn't let me finish.

LYNN
I'm agreeing with you. You didn't. It's not your fault. Now let's get on to my concerns.

LALA
What concerns?

LYNN
You. Here.

LALA
Oh, Lynn. Don't change the subject.

LYNN
It's only fair. You talked about me and all your feelings about my actions. Now I want to talk to you about yours.

LALA
Wait a minute. If this is going to go on for more than a minute, I am going to want a ciggie and maybe some coffee.

LYNN
You just had coffee and a ciggie.

                    LALA
Well, when I hear what you have to say, I
might want more.

*LALA finds her cigarette butt. She checks the
kettle. LYNN begins a search for the coffee
maker.*

                    LYNN
Don't bother, mother. I'll make a pot.

                    LALA
Oh Lynn, you drink so much coffee. I worry
about you.

                    LYNN
I worry about you, mother.

                    LALA
You don't have to worry about me.

                    LYNN
You've have had how many broken ribs in the
past 10 years?

                    LALA
Who's counting?

                    LYNN
Seven. Five that we saw after the fact, in the
past x-rays. And two big stinking whoppers,

including one in which I had to fly in from San
Antonio the day after a three-week trip.
                    LALA
Ah, so you're the one counting.

She does a shot, looks for the bottle.

                    LYNN
I'm counting those, too. That's your one
today. And those ribs, that doesn't even
account for when you broke your leg.

                    LALA
It does, too. That was also a rib. Jenny came
up for that.

                    LYNN
And then I came for the week after Jenny, if
you remember. I think you should move to
San Antonio.

                    LALA
Oh, dear, I don't think so.

                    LYNN
You would like it there.

                    LALA
No, I wouldn't.

                    LYNN
You would have family there.

LALA
You're on the road all the time. See, I do listen.

LYNN
You have several grandchildren there. Including Brendon. And great-grand babies.

LALA
No kidding? Which ones again?

LYNN
Scooter's children.

GREGORY enters with books in his hands.

LYNN (CONT'D)
So you'll think about San Antonio?

LALA
I doubt it.

LYNN
You doubt you'll think about it?

LALA
I doubt I would like it. I don't want to move.

LYNN
You haven't even given it a chance. You might like it.

LALA
I won't ever know, dear. Because I won't do it.

He's about to intercede but holds back.

LYNN
You can't stay here and do nothing. Gregory isn't a solution.

LALA
I'm not doing nothing. It's just my something doesn't seem that exciting.

LYNN
I don't want to come here and find you dead on the floor!

LALA
Oh, darling. You're being melodramatic.

LYNN
I am not. You can't take care of yourself. And Gregory is a 20-something male. He can barely take care of himself.

Now he enters, angry.

GREGORY
I am hard to take care of. I just eat and poop in cycles.

LYNN
Hello, I didn't hear you there.

GREGORY
Obviously.

Despite the tension, they greet.

LYNN
Perhaps you misunderstood what you heard.

GREGORY
Perhaps. And I can't really talk about it now because I have to get some dinner together and go back to the museum.

LALA
Oh, Gregory, you're working again?

GREGORY
Yes, dear. I told you I have to guard at Philipsburg.

LYNN
Can I ask you a favor?

GREGORY
Really?

LYNN
Yes. Would you get my suitcase out of the trunk?

GREGORY
Sure. Nice to know I am good for something.

LYNN
Thank you. It's hard to carry it up the stairs.

He leaves. LALA goes to the living room, finds her cig and another shot. LYNN pours coffee, brings it to LALA.

LALA
Oh, thank you, dear.

LYNN
You're welcome.

LALA
You don't think he heard us, do you?

LYNN
Yes, mother, clearly he did. And if we keep talking now, he will hear us again.

LALA
What do you mean?

LYNN
He's getting my suitcase.

LALA
Oh. Well, perhaps you should say something to him?

LYNN
He's a grown man. I don't have to worry about his feelings.

LALA
You're a grown woman, and I worry about yours.

LYNN
I'm exhausted.

LALA
You see. You work too hard.

GREGORY lugs the suitcase up to a bedroom. He comes down, gets his food.

GREGORY
It's in your room.

LYNN
Thank you.

GREGORY
I don't know what you have in there that's so heavy.

LYNN
My entire life. At least my road life.

GREGORY
How do you move it around when I'm not here?

LYNN
It has wheels. And I tip the porter at the airport.

GREGORY
Alright, then. I've got to go back. I'll be home late.

LALA starts to get up to kiss him.

GREGORY
No, don't get up honey. I'll come to you.

He does. He kisses her on the cheek.

LALA
Goodbye, dear heart. Be safe.

GREGORY
I will. Enjoy your visit.

LALA
I will.

LYNN
I'm making lamb chops tonight.

LALA
Mmmm. One of my favorites. Gregory, do you like lamb chops?

GREGORY
No. Not since I started working at the farm. One of my jobs is to check on the lambs. Anyway, I'll be at work til one.

LYNN
Well, tomorrow I am making meat pie. Do any of the calves have you not eating beef?

GREGORY
No, it sounds great. Anyway, I can't be late.

LALA
Goodbye, darling.

He leaves.

LALA
I think you hurt his feelings.

LYNN
He's a grown man, mother. Anyway why should he be the only one here without hurt feelings?

Act ONE, Scene FOUR

One a.m. LALA is reading the paper. GREGORY enters. He goes to the kitchen to put on the water. LALA appears.

LALA
I didn't realize you were home.

GREGORY
I didn't realize you were up.

LALA
I'm up.

GREGORY
I'm home.

LALA
Oh, Gregory.

GREGORY
Oh, Ga.

LALA
I don't know what to do.

GREGORY
About what?

LALA
Well, Lynn and this bracelet thing for one thing.

GREGORY
I'm not sure what there is you can do.

LALA
Do you think I can ask her to give it back?

GREGORY
Have you?

LALA
Yes.

GREGORY
And did it work?

LALA
No.

GREGORY
Then I'd say no.

LALA
Do you know what gets me so angry?

GREGORY
That you didn't raise her like that?

LALA
Yes. How did you know?

The water boils. He pours it into mugs.

GREGORY
Believe it or not, we've had this conversation before.

LALA
Oh, well, there's no need to rub it in.

GREGORY
I'm not, honey, I'm having a snack before bed. It's late.

LALA

It is?

GREGORY

Yes. It's 1 a.m. After 1 a.m., actually. I had to drive home.

LALA

How far is it?

GREGORY

Which one, Philipsburg or Sunnyside?

LALA

Both.

GREGORY

Sunnyside is about 10 minutes away and Philipsburg is about 20 away, in Sleepy Hollow.

LALA

It didn't used to be called Sleepy Hollow, did it?

GREGORY

No. It used to be North Tarrytown.

LALA

Oh, yes. Why did they change it?

GREGORY
They wanted to take advantage of the tourism.

LALA
Oh, Gregory. What should I do about this thing with Lynn?

GREGORY
I don't know. It is just a bracelet, you know?

LALA fakes a cry. It is over the top.

LALA
But it isn't about the bracelet.

GREGORY
Yes. I know.

LALA
You say it like it isn't important.

GREGORY
I don't mean it that way. I know it is important to you. It's just that it is between you two, and it doesn't concern me. That and it's nearly two in the morning.

LALA
It can't be.

GREGORY
It is. Look.

LALA
Oh, my! Gregory, what am I supposed to do?

Act ONE, Scene FIVE

The next morning. LYNN works in the kitchen. The pashka maker is an elaborate wooden mold. It needs cleaning, assembly.

LYNN
I admit, I was a daddy's girl. I always was. My grandmother, she was a good woman, I thought. She was a hostess. I mean, that's what she did, what she was raised to be. Her father, my mother's grandfather, he was a Polish land baron. To hear mother and grandmother tell the stories.

LALA
He had estates all over, wives and children, too. Every summer we'd wait to find out where we would gather. It was so mysterious. There'd be dozens of children around. Sometimes grandfather would bellow at one of them, "Who's child are you?" And that child would say, "yours, father."

LYNN
I've heard that story a thousand times. Ten thousand times.

LALA
He was Catholic. So, he married frequently.

LYNN

A lot of kids, wives, a lot of people to manage. Bobbi, my grandmother, was the oldest. She became the hostess.

LALA

My grandmother was a gypsy. Romany, I think they prefer. Grandfather saw her one day when she was young, and they fell in love. He asked her parents how much they wanted for her. And they were married. Isn't that romantic?

LYNN

It's like slavery. In my family, three generations ago.

LALA

I think it's romantic. True love. My husband, Irving, he came from a Jewish family. And they never approved of me, but he picked me, and he never let anyone tell him otherwise.

LYNN

I don't believe in love. Romantic love. I tried. My first husband was a louse and a cheat. He was my romantic love. My second, I think I just married him because I wanted another child. Bren. My son. He's my third son. But really, he's my first. All my life, I hated mother playing favorites. I still hate it. Yet, when it comes to my own kids ...

LALA
You can tell yourself who to love, but it doesn't work. Your heart is the only thing you really have to listen to.

LYNN
My grandmother was a hostess. It's the only thing she knew how to do. When she left Russia, when she lost her father, she was left with nothing. She became a stage mom.

LALA
Even at that she wasn't very good.

LYNN
She gave her power to her daughter. For the rest of her life.

LALA
All those nightclubs, all those walks home alone at 11, 12, one in the morning. In Turkey, here in New York, it was scary. A little girl alone on the streets of two of the biggest, most dangerous cities in the world. A little immigrant girl. I barely spoke the languages. I didn't know my way around. But I was the one paying the bills in my family. Where was my mother? She was there, and yet she was never there. But I was better off without her, too.

LYNN
She yelled at Bobbi. Ordered her around. I guess we all did. But I only did it because I saw mother doing it. It doesn't seem right. But that's us. That's what we do. Family.

LALA
You don't pick them. But you do pick them, too.

GREGORY enters, still with bed head, sleep clothes. LALA goes back to sleep.

GREGORY
I see you're back to cooking.

LYNN
You're up early.

GREGORY
Well, you know, I did work until 1 a.m. And then Ga wanted to talk til 2 a.m.

LYNN
I think when you're a certain age, you lose track of time.

GREGORY
Yeah. Teenagers and old folks.

LYNN
How's work?

GREGORY
It's fine. Nice place. Good people. Not sure what I want to do with my life, but I know what I don't. So there's that.

LYNN
You mean journalism? Well, you have lots of questions and no answers.

GREGORY
I guess so.

LYNN
Do you want some breakfast?

GREGORY
No. I'll have a bagel. I got a bunch of stuff at the store before you got here.

LYNN
Yes. Thank you.

GREGORY
I know you think I'm not doing a good job taking care of her.

LYNN
I'm sorry you had to overhear it.

GREGORY
I'm sorry, too, but my point is, I'm here for her.

LYNN
I thought you were here for yourself.

GREGORY
I like being here. Sure.

LYNN
Why not? Close to the city. You live rent free. Expense free.

GREGORY
That's not true. I pay my bills. Car. Insurance. My cobra.

LYNN
That's nice of you.

GREGORY
I pay for the cable. I pay for food.

LYNN
You do?

GREGORY
Yes. I do. It's hard since she tries to stop me, but I do anyway. And when she's short, I buy her vodka and cigarettes.

LYNN
Yes, and I wish you'd stop doing that.

GREGORY
She was drinking and smoking a long time before I got here.

LYNN
Yes, all of my life.

GREGORY
Then don't blame me.

LYNN
I'm not blaming you. I just don't think this is the answer.

GREGORY
Fine. You don't have to think that. But she's not going to San Antonio, and she doesn't want to leave her house.

LYNN
This is not right.

GREGORY
She just wants to talk to you about the bracelet.

LYNN
It's my bracelet!

GREGORY
Look, I don't care about a bracelet. I understand why you wouldn't want it here. But it seems like when she got angry at you

about it, you changed the subject to attack me.

GREGORY

LYNN

I did not.

GREGORY

Well it seems that way to me.

LYNN

I guess that's your problem.

GREGORY

That's my point. Because you've made it my problem.

LYNN

Whose side are you on?

GREGORY

I'm on her side!

LYNN

Well, so am I!

GREGORY

Then stop treating me like we're enemies.

LYNN

Do you know what my biggest fear is? Her, dead on the floor, alone, with no one there to find her for days and days.

GREGORY
Maybe a tad melodramatic?

LYNN
That's my fear. That's all I'm saying.

GREGORY
Fine. But if I'm here, how does that happen?

LYNN
If you're away, with your wrestling.

GREGORY
I don't know where I am with that.

LYNN
Why not?

GREGORY
Well, in part for exactly the reasons you bring up. Plus it's been hard to make contacts here, break in all over again. Anyway, I'm taking an acting class. Maybe it will all have been for a reason, one thing leading to the other. My point is, we're doing the best we can. It's not perfect, but I think it is a lot better with me here than it was without me.

LYNN
I know the answer is yes, but I still do not know.

LALA enters, holding an unlit cig butt.

LALA
You two are so loud you could wake the dead.

LYNN
Mother, what are you doing with that butt?

LALA
Well, I'll tell you what I'm not doing with it. I'm not smoking it because I can't find my lighter.

LYNN
I've got a lighter. I'll trade you for that butt.

LALA
If I give you my butt, I won't need a lighter.

LYNN
I'll give you a new cigarette. But I don't want you smoking butts. Didn't I destroy all your old butts?

LALA
That's what happened to them? So this must be a new butt.

LYNN
Here, I'll trade you.

LYNN hands one to LALA, not releasing until they trade. She shreds the butt.

LALA
I wish you hadn't done that. That was a perfectly good butt.

LYNN
You're going to drive me crazy, mother.

GREGORY
I'm going to go for a run. I'll be back in a hour.

LALA
Oh Gregory, I worry it's too cold outside for you.

GREGORY
I'll bundle up. It helps me break a sweat. And I've got the whole day off, so, it can snow or ice or anything.

LYNN
I hope not. I've got to fly out in the morning.

GREGORY
I work at 9:30 tomorrow so, I could get your bag down tonight.

LYNN
That's fine. My flight is at 10 so I'll be up and out early.

LALA
Oh, Lynn, so soon?

LYNN
Some of us do have to work, Mother.

LYNN
If you're home tonight, I'm making meat and eggplant pies.

GREGORY
Sounds great. Honey, I'll be back soon. I'll bring a paper.

LALA
Oh, Gregory, what would I do without you?

He kisses her on the cheek and leaves.

LYNN
Probably find someone else to enable you.

LALA
I can't believe you're leaving already.

LYNN
I'm not leaving already. I am still here all day today.

LALA
Oh, great, a whole day.

LYNN
A whole day, that I mostly will be spending cooking for you.

LALA
Oh Lynn, you work too hard. Are you coming for Christmas?

LYNN
Not this year. It's hard, mother. Bren's only home a few more years. There's new grand babies. And I'm on the road until then. For Christmas, I want to relax and do nothing.

LALA
I know you. You never do nothing. I worry about you.

LYNN
I worry about you.

LALA
You don't have to worry about me. I'm fine.

Act ONE, Scene SIX

Christmas. Early. There is a nice tree, presents. LALA is sleeping. GREGORY comes downstairs. He goes to the kitchen, makes cocoa, coffee. He brings them into the living room. LALA stirs.

LALA
Oh, darling. I didn't realize you were sitting there.

GREGORY
I didn't want to wake you.

LALA
What time is it?

GREGORY
About 5 a.m.

LALA
5? In the morning? Oh my goodness.

GREGORY
Yes. Well, I have to be at work at 8.

LALA
In the morning? I didn't realize there would be tours today.

GREGORY
There aren't. I'm guarding.

LALA
Oh. On Christmas day, no less.

GREGORY
Yes. But I get double pay. And it is much better than Christmas night. This way I get to be home with you tonight. I made you some coffee.

LALA
Oh, thank you, Gregory.

GREGORY
Are you ready to open presents?

LALA
Should we wait for someone?

GREGORY
There's no one else coming today.

LALA
No one?

GREGORY
No, not today.

LALA
Lynn?

GREGORY
No, she's not coming this year for the holidays.

LALA
Jenny?

GREGORY
She's coming for New Year's. So it's just you and me.

LALA
And you're leaving me, too?

GREGORY
I don't have to leave for more than three hours, and best of all, it is during the day, so I won't be out on a cold Christmas night. And we can have Christmas dinner.

LALA
We can?

GREGORY
Yes. Steve sent a ham.

LALA
Who did?

GREGORY
Steve.

LALA
Your father?

GREGORY
Stepfather.

LALA
Oh, yes. Was he was the one I liked?

GREGORY
I guess.

LALA
I mean, for Jenny. Not that I don't like your father. What happened between them anyway?

GREGORY
Oh, honey, it's ancient history. And how would I know?

LALA
I don't know. You talk to Jenny.

GREGORY
Like my mother. Kids are always the last to know.

LALA
I knew things about my grandfather his wives didn't know. Things about father that mother didn't know. Father liked his girls, his students. They weren't really girls. They were young women. And they loved him. He was better teaching them horse riding than he was training a group of Cossacks.

GREGORY
I had no idea.

LALA
Neither did mother. Father died on Thanksgiving. I've always hated it since.

GREGORY
Why don't we open some presents?

LALA
I don't know if we have any.

GREGORY
We have plenty. See?

LALA
Oh. I don't remember getting all of those.

GREGORY
You didn't. I did.

LALA
Oh. I didn't want you to spend your own money on them.

GREGORY
You gave me money. But I spent my money on your presents.

LALA
You did?

LALA begins to cry.

GREGORY
What?

LALA
I didn't get anything for you.

GREGORY
No, honey, you did.

LALA
I did?

GREGORY
Yes. See?

He shows her a big present.

GREGORY
To Gregory, from Ga.

LALA
I got that? For you?

GREGORY
Yes. Of course, Santa helped a bit, but you paid for it.

LALA
Oh. Wow. I can't wait to see what I got you.

They laugh. GREGORY picks out a long, narrow one. He hands it to LALA.

LALA
Is this for me or for me to give to you?

GREGORY
That's for you. Forgive me for being practical.

                    LALA
Oh, boy.

LALA opens it. It is a carton of Parliament Lights. She claps.

                LALA (CONT'D)
A wealth! I have a wealth.

                  GREGORY
May your daughters forgive me.

                    LALA
Oh. Don't listen to them. Now if only I had some vodka.

                  GREGORY
You have a full bottle, honey. They delivered two days ago.

                    LALA
Is it still full?

                  GREGORY
No. But it is three quarters full.

                    LALA
Oh. That's a lot.

                  GREGORY
It is. And you have a full shot glass over there.

LALA takes a sip from her shot glass.

LALA
Where are my manners. Gregory, do you want a drink?

GREGORY
No, thank you. It's early, and I have to work later.

LALA
Oh. That's right. Well, I'll have one. I can always take a nap after you leave.

GREGORY
Okay, here's one from you to me.

LALA
Oooh. That's a big one. I can't wait to see what it is. And Gregory? I paid for it? You didn't pay for your own gift?

GREGORY
No, honey, I didn't. Oh, Ga, it's just what I wanted.

LALA
That was good of me. What is it?

GREGORY
It's an easel. For painting.

LALA
I didn't know you painted.

GREGORY
I don't. I mean, I didn't. But I think I'd like to. Being at the museums. Seeing the Artists on the Hudson.

LALA
What was that?

GREGORY
Something we had at one of the museums.

LALA
Philipsburg?

GREGORY
No, Sunnyside.

LALA
Sunnyside. Funny name.

GREGORY
It's wonderful.

LALA
I'm glad you like it. I wish I'd gotten you paint or brushes.

GREGORY
I have some more presents over there.

LALA
You do? Oh, Gregory.

GREGORY
But first one for you.

He hands her a small package to open.

LALA
Oh, Gregory. Lighters! Wow, how many is that? One, two, three, four, five, six. Six! That's a lot of lighters.

GREGORY
You need lighters.

LALA
I need one. Maybe two so I don't have to go back and forth looking for one. But six is too many. Have one.

GREGORY
I will take one, but I want you to have one in each room. Lori said she smelled gas the other day, and that you had left one of the burners on.

LALA
I did not. Who is this woman you speak of?

GREGORY
Lori, the tenant upstairs.

LALA
She must be wrong. Is she a liar? I don't know the tenants as well as I used to.

GREGORY
No, she's cute.

LALA
Oh, then your instincts are too messed up to judge.

GREGORY
She meant well. She was worried. Everyone knows you use the stove if you can't find a lighter or matches.

LALA
You should have given me matches, too.

GREGORY
There's more presents.

He gets up, walks some of the lighters around, one on each table and one to the other rooms. She follows.

LALA
Oh, Gregory! If you're going that way, maybe you could put the water on.

GREGORY
Of course I will. We have some treats, too. Turnovers, crumb cakes, cheese Danishes. All the stuff you like.

LALA
Oh, boy. But what about the other presents?

GREGORY
We have time. We have lots of time.

In the kitchen, he puts on the water. He offers her a Danish.

LALA
Mmm. This is good. Have some.

GREGORY
I've got a bagel and some cream cheese.

LALA
That's good, too.

GREGORY
Merry Christmas, honey.

LALA
Merry Christmas, darling. So when are you going to work?

GREGORY
About three hours.

LALA
Are there any tenants here?

GREGORY
I don't think so. Maybe Chevonne, if she's just going to see her parents during the day.

LALA
She's nice.

GREGORY
They're all nice. Even Lori.

LALA
Who?

GREGORY
The girl who told me about the gas.

LALA
Oh. You do seem to think that. I think Jenny is seeing a fellow. Do you know about this?

GREGORY
Yes. Well, she's bringing him to Christmas.

LALA
Today?

GREGORY
No. Not today. Russian Christmas.

LALA

Oh, Russian Christmas. When is that?

GREGORY
Well, judging from my childhood, it is whenever someone who wasn't there for Christmas is there after Christmas. In this case, I think next week.

LALA
When next week?

GREGORY
This time next week. For New Year's.

LALA
Oh. That's not real Russian Christmas.

GREGORY
No. Not really. That's what I mean. Anyway, they're coming for New Year's. They want to see you for the millennium.

LALA
The what?

GREGORY
The millennium. You know, the start of the new century.

LALA
Ah. But back to Jenny for a minute. Do you know anything about this fellow she's seeing?

GREGORY

No. Not any more than you do.

LALA
Oh. But they're coming here?

GREGORY
Yes. Next week. You ready to open some more presents?

LALA
In a minute. I want to ask you about this fellow she's with.

GREGORY
You make it sound like she's 15, but yes.

LALA
Is he black?

GREGORY
Is he what?

LALA
I get the feeling he's black or something.

GREGORY
You get the feeling he's black. Or something?

LALA
Yes. Do you know why I would think that?

GREGORY

Well, for starters, I think he is.

LALA
Black?

GREGORY
Yes. Not or something though.

LALA
You're making fun of me.

GREGORY
Just a little. Yes.

LALA
Well, it's not nice.

GREGORY
I'm sorry. To be honest, I don't know much more than you.

LALA
Do you know where she met this fellow?

GREGORY
At a meeting.

LALA
A business meeting?

GREGORY
No. A different kind of meeting.

LALA

Like what?

GREGORY
AA, ACOA, something like that.

LALA
I worry. I mean about Jenny.

GREGORY
I know. But she is in her 50s, you know?

LALA
Yes, but she's Jenny. She never was good at taking care of herself. She was only 10 when her father died. You never met him did you?

GREGORY
No. Mom was 10, remember?

LALA
You would have liked him. And he would have gotten a kick out of you, too. Especially now. I mean, he would have liked you when you were a kid. But he would have appreciated you as a writer. Or acting, if that's what you are going to do. Is that what you are going to do?

GREGORY
I don't know.

LALA

Because I'm just not sure about this wrestling ... thing.

GREGORY
Yes, honey, I know.

LALA
It's just so barbaric. And you are not barbaric.

GREGORY
I know. Anyway, it isn't really much of an issue since I haven't had a match in months. I can't make connections here. I left them in Alabama. Anyway, there are other things here. Like acting. It seems like a straight line to acting.

LALA
So you're a ham?

GREGORY
A what?

LALA
You know, it's what they call actors.

GREGORY
Oh. Yes. I guess. We'll see.

LALA
It's too bad your father wasn't still alive. If he were still at the Music Hall, he could really help you. And I would call someone there, but

the people he knew are all gone now. I mean, it's been 30, 40 years. Oh, well.

GREGORY
Hey, are you ready for those presents now?

LALA
Yes. Let me just get my ciggies. Do I have any ciggies?

Act ONE, Scene SEVEN

One week later. GREGORY and LALA sit with JENNY and LAWRENCE, a black man, 50s, tall, weathered. He is nervous.

JENNY
Okay, one more for each of you.

LALA
Oh, Jenny, you did too much.

JENNY
Very little. Not much at all. And a week late to boot.

LALA
Russian Christmas, darling.

JENNY
Here, Mom, for you, from both of us.
LAWRENCE hands her an oddly shaped package. She opens it to reveal.

LALA
Oh, Jenny! Vodka.

LAWRENCE
Good vodka. Or so I'm told. I haven't had any.

LALA
Well, we can all have a drink. Where is my shot glass?

GREGORY
Right there on the table, Ga.

LALA
Oh, well, don't rub it in.

GREGORY
I wasn't.

JENNY
Here, I'll get ones for all of us.

GREGORY
They met in group. Clearly it hadn't taken.

JENNY
I'll pour one for everyone. Gregory, do you want one, too?

GREGORY
Yes. I'll have one.

She passes them out. They toast.

LAWRENCE
To family.

ALL
To family!

LALA
You know, I think he looks like Fedya.

LAWRENCE
Me?

LALA
Yes.

LAWRENCE
Who is that?

JENNY
Uncle Fedya. A relative of my mom's from Russia.

LALA
He moved to New York, like all of all. Don't you think he looks like Fedya?

They all laugh nervously.

JENNY
Yes. Sort of. Okay, one for Gregory.

She hands him one. He opens it. A book.

GREGORY
The Artist's Way. Cool. Thanks.

LALA
Oooh, what is that?

JENNY
A book for budding creative types.

LALA
That's my Gregory.

JENNY
Lawrence has another one for you. Why don't you guys get it?

LAWRENCE
Where is it?

JENNY
I think I left it in the other room.

They walk to the other room. LAWRENCE hands him a small gift bag.

JENNY
Thank you for having us here, Mom.

LALA

Oh, Jenny, you're always welcome here. You know that.

GREGORY

Oh wow, it's a, what do you call it?

LAWRENCE

It's an incense burner. And there's something inside.

He opens it. There are two small baggies inside, the size of dime bags.

GREGORY

Oh, my goodness!

JENNY

Thank you for being welcoming of Lawrence.

LALA

Oh, Jenny. You know you are always welcome here.

LAWRENCE

Your mom said you would like this. That it would be okay.

GREGORY

Yeah, it's great. I almost got some for you guys, in Washington Square Park. But they seem to think I'm a cop.

LAWRENCE
I would think that, too. If it were me on the street.

GREGORY
Yeah. I'm, uh, thank you.

LAWRENCE
I was thinking maybe you'd have a drink with me, too. While we're here. We stopped off at a bar up the street.

GREGORY
The pub.

LAWRENCE
Yes. The pub. It seems like a nice place.

GREGORY
Well, I have to guard tonight.

LAWRENCE
On New Year's Eve?

GREGORY
I know. I lead a glamorous life. And then from 8-4 tomorrow. But tomorrow night, if they are open? For the football game?

LAWRENCE
Sounds good. Hey, Jennifer. I think he likes it.

LAWRENCE walks back to the living room.

GREGORY
The thing about being an enabler is, you're enabling one another. And unless you're a hypocrite, you know it.

GREGORY rejoins the group.

LALA
Oh, Jenny, this is wonderful!

JENNY
I'm glad you like it.

GREGORY
What is it, Ga?

She holds up a book for him to see.

LALA
It's a Pushkin. A nice one. He was a great Russian writer. Oh, that's great. Oh, Jenny, the illustrations are beautiful. Look at this? Where ever did you find this?

JENNY
It turns out there's a Russian bookstore in Rockville.

LALA
Well, it is just wonderful.

LAWRENCE
Did you give him the other one?

JENNY
No, not yet, dear. He was over there with you.

JENNY hands him a small square package.

GREGORY
Oh, my goodness.

LALA
What is it?

JENNY
It's a cell phone. For Gregory. So he can find out about auditions wherever he is. And he can stay in touch with you.

GREGORY
Thank you.

LAWRENCE
We got it from the store where I work. It's a basic model.

GREGORY
It's great.

JENNY
We got you a local number. I wrote it down. And I'm going to pay the monthly service for you.

GREGORY
Wow. You don't have to do that.

JENNY
I know, but it'll make it easier for you to check on Ga. For her to feel better, or get you in an emergency. That's big.

LALA starts to cry.

JENNY
Mother, what's wrong?

LALA
I don't have anything for you. I didn't get you any presents.

GREGORY
That's not true, Ga. We have something for them over here.

LALA
Oh, good. I don't remember getting anything.

GREGORY
Oh, honey, of course you got something. Look, here they are. Let's begin, shall we.

LALA
Let's. I can't wait to see what they are.

JENNY
Where did that easel come from?

GREGORY
It was Ga's gift to me.

LAWRENCE
It's nice.

GREGORY
It's basic, but I like it.

LAWRENCE
Is that your painting?

GREGORY
Yes, one of my first. It's just an attempt. I don't really know how to paint.

LAWRENCE
No, I like it. It says something.

GREGORY
Yeah, it does. It says I don't know how to paint.

LAWRENCE
No. Something more. Jenny, what do you think?

JENNY
Well, it's, um ... it is very dark.

END OF ACT ONE

Act TWO, Scene ONE

Late night/early morning. The house is quiet, dark. Everyone sleeps. Lala has nightmares. Lights flash; a storm rages.

LALA
Irving. Oh, Irving. Why did you leave me. Irving. IRVING!

Doors slam. People appear, disappear.

LYNN
You're in danger, mother!

LALA
But Lynn!

LYNN
I can't talk now. I have to go.

JENNY
I worry about you, mother.

LALA
I worry about you.

JENNY
Oh, mother, don't be silly.

GREGORY
Can it wait? I'm late for work.

LALA
When will you be back?

GREGORY
There's a note by the phone.

LALA
Oh, grandfather, what happened to you?

GREGORY
Hi, honey. I'm back. But now I've got class in the city.

LYNN
You smoke too much mother.

JENNY
You drink too much mother.

LAWRENCE
I'm going to hurt your daughter!

LALA
Don't kill grandfather!

LYNN
I've got to go.

JENNY
I've got to go.

GREGORY
I'll be home about midnight.

LALA
Don't hurt me! I'm just a little girl.

GREGORY
Can we talk about this later?

LYNN
I don't want to talk about it.

JENNY
We've already had this conversation.

LALA
No. No. NOOOOO!

She stands and screams then crumples to the ground. GREGORY rushes in.

GREGORY
Oh my God! Ga! Are you alright?

LALA
Oh, Gregory, I'm ... can you help me up?

He helps her to the couch. She screams; every inch is a battle.

LALA (CONT'D)
Easy. Easy.

GREGORY
I'm going as easy as I can, honey./What is it?

LALA
Oh, such pain./My side!

He sets her down. Every move hurts.

GREGORY
Oh, God. Does it feel like a lung?

LALA
No. Lower.

GREGORY
Where? That's not what I was expecting.

LALA
What were you Ouch! expect-UG-ing?

GREGORY
Organs.

LALA
Gregory, it hurts!

GREGORY
I know. It's probably a rib.

LALA
How do you, OH, know?

GREGORY
You've broken ribs before.

LALA
But I didn't do anything. I was sleeping. And then I woke up on the floor in pain.

GREGORY
Maybe you hurt it falling to the floor.

LALA
It hurts.

GREGORY
Here. I've got some Tiger Balm. Where does it hurt?

LALA
My side.

GREGORY
Point to it.

He lifts her gown and puts on lots of Tiger Balm. She oohs as it tingles.

LALA
It tingles.

GREGORY
Good. Let me get you a couple of aspirin.

LALA
Well, maybe just one.

GREGORY
Honey, you're in crying pain. I think you could take two!

LALA
Well, maybe two. And maybe some tea, please.

He rushes to the kitchen, puts on the tea, grabs aspirin, water. Rushes back.

LALA
Gregory, it hurts.

GREGORY
I know. Here, here's the aspirin and some water.

She takes one, sets one on her table.

LALA
I'll save the other one in case I need it later.

GREGORY
We have more. I'll put more out in case it hurts overnight.

LALA
What time is it?

GREGORY
Three a.m.

LALA
I'm sorry.

GREGORY
Don't be sorry. Are you okay?

LALA
If I don't move.

GREGORY
Let me go get your tea.

LALA
Oh, that would be nice.

He leaves. She moans. He stops at the stairs, thinking, darts up to his room. He finds a small pipe and one of the dime bags. He loads the pipe. Her cries of pain continue. He runs downstairs to the kitchen. He brings her the tea.

GREGORY
Here you go. Sugar and lemon as you like it.

LALA
Oh, thank you Gregory.

GREGORY
You're welcome. Are you alright? Should I call an ambulance?

LALA
No, but maybe we should call the doctor.

GREGORY
At 3 a.m.? We'd have to go to the emergency room.

LALA
No. In the morning. Maybe he can prescribe something.

GREGORY
We could go to the hospital! We should, honey.

LALA
I don't know that they can do anything.

GREGORY
They can do something for your pain.

LALA
Gregory, I said no! I'm sorry darling. I didn't mean to snap.

GREGORY
That's okay. I'm just trying to help, and I don't know how.

LALA
You are helping. Could you find me my cigarettes?

GREGORY
Yes. I think they're in the kitchen.

GREGORY goes to the kitchen. He finds cigarettes. She cries out again. He pulls the pipe out, lights it and takes a big draw. He enters the living room and lights a cigarette. He hands it to her and exhales. The room fills with smoke. She relaxes.

LALA
That tea really helps.

He goes down the hall and does it again. He comes back, lets out a big puff, right in her face. She coughs.

GREGORY
Oops. Sorry.

LALA
I don't mind.

GREGORY
How do you feel?

LALA
Better. Is there anything to eat?

GREGORY
Yes. I'll get you something. You only took one aspirin.

LALA
I'll save the other for later. I'm sorry to be such a bother.

GREGORY
You're not a bother.

LALA
The thing is, I didn't do anything.

GREGORY
I know. Here, I'll be right back with your turnover.

He goes to the kitchen, does the smoking thing again. Exhales.

GREGORY
I know how it looks. But what do I do, let her suffer? She won't go to the hospital, and the last time she did, her leg muscles shrunk so bad she was in a home for weeks. Other things, she can handle. The home nearly killed her.

Realizing what he has done, he repeats his cycle and then brings her the food.

LALA
Oh, thank you, darling.

GREGORY
Of course, honey.

LALA
Do you see the remote?

GREGORY
Yes. It's here. Not much on at 4 in the morning though.

LALA
Oh goodness, it isn't that early! Is it? Well, just put it on channel two, and something will come on. You should get some more rest.

GREGORY
I will. Luckily, I don't work today. So I'll be around to make sure you're okay.

LALA
That's good.

GREGORY
I have class tonight, but if you're still in pain I won't go.

LALA
What class are you taking again?

GREGORY
Acting class. In the city.

As she talks, he goes to his easel.

LALA

Oh, that's right. You're a ham. Oh, I wish your father was here. He would be able to help. And the thing is, there isn't even anybody for me to call that's still at the music hall. Gregory, I wanted to ask you something. What do you think of this fellow Jenny brought here. What was his name? Larry?

GREGORY

Lawrence.

LALA

Yes. That's it. I don't know about him.

GREGORY

What's to know?

LALA

Where did he come from?

GREGORY

Well, I think he's from Maryland. Or D.C.

LALA

But I mean, who is he? How did they meet? What does he do?

GREGORY

They met in group.

LALA

What kind of group?

GREGORY
Like AA.

LALA
Like what?

GREGORY
A therapy group.

LALA
I worry about Jenny. What do you think of this fellow?

GREGORY
I don't know.

LALA
What do you mean you don't know?

GREGORY
I don't know, honey. I'm trying not to think about it.

LALA
That's a fine thing.

GREGORY
I know. And it's late, and I was worried about you, you know?

LALA
You don't have to worry about me.

GREGORY
It's four in the morning, and we're up because you woke up screaming, remember?

LALA
Yes. Vaguely.

GREGORY
Sorry. Honestly, I don't know what to think of him.

LALA
Do you like him?

GREGORY
I'm trying to like him. I want to like him. I want to think everything is okay in my mother's life, you know?

LALA
I do know. That's how I feel about my daughter. But you don't, do you?

GREGORY
Don't know how I feel?

LALA
No. Don't like him.

GREGORY
All I can say is, I don't know.

LALA
Yeah, well, me neither.

He paints. LALA is soon asleep.

GREGORY
I was lying. I did know. I tried to like him. I wanted to like him. All I know is I felt unsettled. When you meet someone in group, you probably shouldn't invite their son out for a drink and bring him weed. And I gladly accepted it ... the weed, if not the drink. Later my mom admitted they had been using harder drugs, too. And he had been abusive. I felt awful. Luckily, my grandmother never knew. From the time of my mom's divorce from my step-dad, my mom became a mystery to me. The fog of the pills, then the rehab, then the distance, not just the 1,000 miles to Alabama, but a different kind of distance. It makes me feel ... depressed to think about. My grandmother always said she worried about my mom, and eventually, she passed the worry down to me. You're not supposed to worry about your parents. Maybe that's the door to adulthood; the day you start worrying about your parents. *(He makes sure LALA is sleeping and takes the pipe out for another hit.)* Who am I to talk? To judge? That's what I wonder.

Act TWO, Scene TWO

Two months later. GREGORY is asleep. LALA is smoking and drinking coffee.

LALA

My father was a horseman, by blood. His name, Selihov, well hov was Russian for Khan. He came from the Khan, from someone named Seli Khan, as Gregory would say. That's what my grandmother would tell us. And the thing is, oh my ...

She abruptly gets up and hurries out of the room, but does not make it to the stairs. With as much dignity as possible, she drips fecal matter.

LALA (CONT'D)

Oh Lala, what have you done? Hello? HELLO! Is anyone home?

She continues to work toward the bathroom. GREGORY is in bed.

LALA (CONT'D)

Gregory! Greg-ory! Oh dear, please wake up.

He wakes, confused. He leaps out of bed, wearing nothing but boxer shorts.

GREGORY

Honey! What's wrong!

LALA
No, need to scream, I'm right here.

GREGORY
Oh thank God. You're okay.

LALA
But I'm not. I need your help. I'm sorry to wake you darling, but I didn't remember if you were home, and oh, uh oh, I've got to go to the bathroom. Can you get dressed and I'll show you the problem?

He puts on sweats and a t-shirt. He enters the hall and smells the problem.

GREGORY
Oh. God. No wonder she was screaming. This is ... (He gags).

He follows the trail. He goes to the kitchen and gets paper towels, a bucket of soapy water.

LALA
Oh darling, I'm so sorry.

GREGORY
You don't have to be sorry.

LALA
Easy for you to say.

GREGORY
Yes, easy. Oh, yuck.

He gags as he picks up a clump.

LALA
Oh, come on, it's not that bad. You're putting it on thick.

He runs up and flushes it.

GREGORY
Oh, honey, it's on your ... we need to clean you up.

LALA
Oh, Gregory, I'm a mess.

She gives out a fake cry.

GREGORY
It's okay. Why don't you go back to the bathroom and get undressed, and I'll get you some clean clothes.

She goes to the bathroom. He runs down and gets a new gown, underpants and bathrobe, from the living room. He returns, knocks on the bathroom.

LALA
Gregory! Don't come in yet.

GREGORY
I have clean clothes.

LALA
Well, I'm having trouble getting clean.

GREGORY
I can help.

LALA
I don't want you to see me like this.

GREGORY
It's okay. Put a towel on, and I'll just help you clean.

She steps out in a towel. He takes paper towels, cleans her legs, feet.

LALA
Oh, Gregory.

GREGORY
Oh, Lala.

LALA
I'm a mess.

GREGORY
Nope. You're all clean again. There's a couple more, so you can clean the rest of you. Here's clean underwear, a clean slip and

your zip up robe. Where are your dirty clothes?

LALA
In here.

GREGORY
I'll take those and get them in the wash. Anything else?

LALA
Isn't that enough?

GREGORY
I suppose so.

LALA
This is hard work. I need to rest.

GREGORY
Is your stomach okay?

LALA
Yes. Why?

GREGORY
Oh, no reason. But if you're still having problems, you can lay down in your bedroom, and then it won't be such a walk.

LALA
Yes. This has me winded. But there's more to clean.

GREGORY
Don't worry. I can do it.

LALA
Will you be here?

GREGORY
I have to work today, but not until 10:30. The good thing is, that's six hours until I have to work.

LALA
Sunnyside?

GREGORY
Yes, and I only work til five so I'll be here tonight. So, you'll sleep up here?

LALA
Yes.

GREGORY
Can I bring anything up for you?

LALA
Oh, nothing. Maybe some tea. And my ciggies. And some matches or something. And do we have any vodka?

GREGORY
Maybe that's not the best thing for your stomach right now.

LALA
No, probably not. But do we have any? Or need any?

GREGORY
We have some. Why don't you lie down? I'll get you tea and ciggies?

LALA
I'm a mess.

GREGORY
No, you're not.

LALA
I need to do something about me.

GREGORY
Well, you can start by going into your seldom used bedroom and getting some rest.

ACT TWO, Scene THREE

Six months later. GREGORY is downstairs, painting. LALA sleeps on the couch. The TV is on.

GREGORY
It went like that for the year. Broken ribs. Hospital visits. Stray poop. Dirty nightgowns. And then lots of good times. Fun. Love. Dinners. Coffee. In between my work, classes, auditions and limited social life.

Even a limited social life made me feel guilty. I mean, who was I to have a life when/

LALA is waking, watches him painting.

LALA
Gregory? Is that you?

GREGORY
Yes, honey.

LALA
Are you leaving?

GREGORY
Yes. But just for the week.

LALA
A whole week? Oh, Gregory. Where are you going?

GREGORY
To my sister's wedding, in Virginia.

LALA
You mean, what is her name?

GREGORY
Tiffany. Beverly's daughter. My father's ex-wife's daughter.

LALA
Oh, yes. They came here once. She was blond. Very pretty. What happened to them?

GREGORY
She was cheating on him.

LALA
Oh, I'm sorry.

GREGORY
I was never a big fan of hers anyway.

LALA
Did she get married before?

GREGORY
Beverly?

LALA
Yes. I mean, no, your sister.

GREGORY
Yes. This is her second marriage.

LALA
How do you feel about that?

GREGORY
I don't know. I liked her first husband. I haven't met this one. I don't know what to expect. She's, um, complicated.

LALA
Oh. Why?

GREGORY
I don't know. Troubled. Sort of wild. Father issues. We have a history.

LALA
I thought she was, I don't know, the opposite of that.

GREGORY
That's her older sister, Melissa.

LALA
Oh. That's right. I forget.

GREGORY
I'm going early to go to Ocracoke and then the wedding.

LALA
That's where Jenny and Steve used to go in the summers. Is it close to the wedding?

GREGORY
A few hours. But I am going there first and then driving up.

LALA
It sounds fun.

GREGORY
I don't know about the wedding, but the week overall will be.

LALA
I hope it is fun. It's good for you to have some fun. Not have to worry about your old grandmither.

GREGORY
I still worry. Just less. I know someone else is helping you.

LALA
Is someone else coming?

GREGORY
Yes. Mom tonight and then Lynn at the end of the week.

LALA
My goodness. Both of my daughters! Together?

GREGORY
Not together, but both this week.

LALA
A wealth. When are you going?

GREGORY
Soon. After I shower and pack.

LALA
What about my vodka and ciggies?

GREGORY
What about them?

LALA
I don't have any.

GREGORY
You do. I got a fresh carton of cigs yesterday, and they delivered a bottle of vodka two days ago.

LALA
Oh, good.

GREGORY
I'm going to shower. Do you want anything?

LALA
Some coffee and something to eat. Nothing big. Just a taste.

GREGORY
You got it.

The lights change. LALA is sleeping. She wakes up in a fit.

LALA
Gregory. GREGory. Are you here? Oh goodness, where did you go? Jenny, JEN-ny.

Is anybody here? I must have a butt somewhere. Where is everybody? Is anybody here?

She stands again, but can't manage, collapses on the couch. The lights change, the winds pick up.

LYNN is in the kitchen.

          LYNN
Mother! I worry about you.

JENNY is in a bedroom.

          JENNY
Mom, I'm fine.

          LYNN
Mother, you have to come to San Antonio.

GREGORY at his easel but still distant.

          GREGORY
Ga, I gotta go to work.

          LYNN
Mother I don't want to talk about it.

          GREGORY
I left you a note.

JENNY
Mother, you smoke too much.

GREGORY
You have cigarettes. There's a box of matches.

LYNN
Mother, stop smoking those butts!

LALA
I have a wealth of butts!

LYNN
Not anymore you don't!

LALA
No!

GREGORY
You can't be out of vodka, we just got some the other day.

JENNY
Mother, I worry about your drinking.

LALA
Jenny, I worry about you!

LYNN
Mother, stop smoking!

JENNY
Mother, I'm capable of taking care of myself.

GREGORY
I'll be home at midnight.

LYNN
I'll be back in October.

JENNY
I'll see you for Christmas.

LALA
But I need somebody now! Gregory? Jenny? Lynn? Debbie? Wait, who is Debbie? Irving? Oh, Irving why did you leave me?

LALA screams and collapses. Lights return to normal. JENNY enters.

JENNY
Mother? Mom, I'm here. Mother? Oh God.

She rushes to her. LALA is awake and lifts her head, but she is not well.

LALA
Oh, Jenny. I'm so glad you're here.

JENNY
Mother, you are burning up. Are you okay?

LALA
You know, I'm not sure.

END OF ACT TWO

Act THREE, Scene ONE

The living room has changed. There's a hospital-style bed dominating the room. An oxygen tank is next to the bed. Lala is in the bed. She is frail.

LALA
Hello, is anybody here? Jenny? Gregory?

DEBBIE WHEELER is a 48-year old black woman. She is round but not obese.

DEBBIE
Hello.

LALA
Hello. Who are you?

DEBBIE
I'm Debbie. We met yesterday.

LALA
We did?

DEBBIE
Yes.

LALA
Oh, my head. Is anybody else here?

DEBBIE
Not all the cars are here, but I just got here so I am not sure. I made you some coffee.

LALA
You did?

DEBBIE
Yes. Jenny said you like coffee and Danish when you wake up.

LALA
Oh, that was nice of her. And you, too. What did you say your name was?

DEBBIE
Debbie. And it still is, too.

LALA
Thank you, Debbie. But I don't know what happen to my stuff.

DEBBIE
What stuff?

LALA
Well, my table and the things on it. My glasses. The remote. My cigarettes and vodka.

DEBBIE
I thought you meant important stuff.

LALA
That's very important stuff!

DEBBIE
I know it is. I have to talk to Jenny about it.

LALA
Who?

DEBBIE
Your daughter. Jenny.

JENNY enters, in sleep clothes. She has cigs with her, but thinks to hide them.

JENNY
Talk to me about what?

LALA
Oh, Jenny, I am glad you are here. How long are you staying?

JENNY
I'm here Mom. I'm not leaving.

LALA
For good?

JENNY
Yes. For good. I mean, I still have a trial or two in Maryland, but other than that I am staying here.

LALA
Oh, Jenny! I'm so happy.

JENNY
I'm glad.

LALA
And what about that fellow? I don't remember his name.

JENNY
Lawrence?

LALA
I don't remember.

JENNY
Can you describe him?

LALA
Not in front of Debbie.

JENNY
It's okay, Mother. (To Debbie) Lawrence was black.

DEBBIE
Really? Oh Jenny! We have to talk. Do you like mudslides?

JENNY
I don't know if I've ever had one.

DEBBIE
You have to try one. We'll have mudslides and talk.

LALA
Um, excuse me, I don't mean to break up this pow wow, here, but what about me?

DEBBIE
Lala, I thought vodka was your thing?

LALA
That's what I mean. Has anybody seen my vodka and ciggies?

DEBBIE
Well, I'm going to go get that coffee for you.

LALA
Oh good. In the meantime, what about my vodka and ciggies?

JENNY
I've got them, mother, but we have to have a talk about them.

LALA
Yes, let's have a talk.

JENNY
As your nurse, Debbie might have something to say.

LALA
That is funny because she said I should talk to you.

JENNY
I'll talk to her, and we'll get back to you.

LALA
When?

JENNY
How about now?

LALA
I would like that.

JENNY goes to the kitchen. To her surprise, DEBBIE is doing dishes.

JENNY
You don't have to do that.

DEBBIE
I know I don't.

JENNY
They tell us not to ask you to do chores.

DEBBIE
They tell us not to do chores. But I'm here for eight hours a day. What am I going to do, sit and watch TV all day?

JENNY
The temp we had before you did.

DEBBIE
A lot of the nurses do. Or talk on their phones. I'd rather work in a clean house. Not that it was dirty.

JENNY
You can say it. There are cobwebs older than my son.

DEBBIE
With an old woman and a young man things didn't get cleaned much. I'm sure they did their best.

JENNY
Young men are not the cleanest things in the world, are they?

DEBBIE
Jenny, my son, Travis, thinks dirt just appears and disappears by the hand of God. And I'm

afraid to tell him otherwise because it's the only time he ever mentions God.

LALA
I hate to break up all that laughter in there, but isn't anyone supposed to be helping me.

JENNY
Just a minute, Mother, we're still discussing things.

LALA
It isn't my hearing that isn't working, darling. I know you weren't discussing me.

JENNY
I swear that woman has selective hearing. She hasn't heard a word my nephew or stepson has ever said, but she knows when we aren't discussing what she wants us to talk about.

LALA
What's that darling?

JENNY
Nothing mother.

DEBBIE
What was it we were supposed to be discussing?

JENNY
Her vodka and cigarettes.

DEBBIE
I told her to talk to you about it.

JENNY
Yes, and I told her to talk to you about it. So maybe we should talk to each other. What do you think?

DEBBIE
Jenny, here's the thing. And I'm telling you this as a nurse who always has older patients. Do you know how many I save?

JENNY
Not many?

DEBBIE
Not any. You know, that doesn't mean we can't prolong her life, and give her an enjoyable life while she's here.

JENNY
What about the oxygen?

DEBBIE
Oh. We can turn that off.

JENNY
Well, you know, they tell you it could explode.

DEBBIE
Jenny, I didn't survive two bad husbands and a lifetime in the Bronx to get blown up in Westchester in some white woman's oxygen explosion. I'll show you how to turn off the oxygen.

Lights down. Lights up.

LALA
Hello, is anyone here?

GREGORY
I'm right here, honey.

LALA
Oh, I thought you were, what's her name?

GREGORY
Debbie.

LALA
That's right. Where is she?

GREGORY
It's six. She went home at five.

LALA
I like her.

GREGORY
I hear she lets you turn off the oxygen and have a cigarette.

LALA

I like that.

GREGORY

Yes. As long as we don't blow the place up.

LALA

No. That would be bad. (Beat) Do you know where Jenny is?

GREGORY

She went out to do some food shopping.

LALA

Do you know what she's doing here?

GREGORY

She's living.

LALA

She's staying? Here? With me? With us?

GREGORY

Yes.

LALA

Oh, Gregory. That's so wonderful. What about that fellow? I can't remember his name. The one that was here that time.

GREGORY

Lawrence?

LALA
I think so.

GREGORY
She said he went to a program in Buffalo, and she told him she was moving here and wasn't going back with him.

LALA
He doesn't think he's coming here does he?

GREGORY
No. He isn't moving here. It is just us. And the tenants. And Debbie.

LALA
How nice. Say what do you think about this Debbie woman, and her friend she brought? I think her name is Lily?

Lights down. Lights up. Night.

LALA
So I can't smoke or drink when I want to. But weirder still is I no longer walk. Me, a dancer. How could my legs not work? Jenny and Debbie remind me I refused to go to rehab. How was I to know? It's weird being up late. I've been up at all hours of the night for 40 years since Irving died. Now I'm hardly up late at all. Somehow I fall asleep and then it's four or five a.m. If someone isn't here, I call and call until they arrive. Jenny sleeps the

soundest. She always did. Gregory is quicker but grumpier. He said something about going to film school. I'd like to go to film school. I'd like to do a lot of things I didn't get to do. I guess I did a lot. And then Irving died. I guess he ... I guess I ... all my relatives said, "you have to sell the house. You have to sell the house." But where would I have been then? Where would we all be?

A light goes on upstairs, above LALA's area. JENNY's space. JENNY is in the chair, asleep, a book in her lap. A knock on her door. GREGORY peaks in.

GREGORY
Hey, are you asleep?

JENNY
No. I mean, I was, but I was trying to read. Drifting off.

GREGORY
If you want to sleep …

JENNY
No. That's okay. Did you get it?

GREGORY
Yeah before class. Although for some reason it is harder and harder to hook up with my buddy, Jordan.

JENNY
But you did?

He reaches into his pocket and pulls out a bag. He hands it to her.

JENNY
Wow. Cool. That was $50?

GREGORY
It was. New York City delivery prices. They call it Max Green.

JENNY
No, it's good. Smells good. And they bring it right to you?

GREGORY
Yeah. Delivery. They go anywhere in Manhattan and Brooklyn.

JENNY
Where's the pipe?

GREGORY
I don't know. I looked in my room but it wasn't there.

She roots around, finds it.

JENNY
Oh, here it is.

She opens the bag, takes a little bit out and loads the pipe. Looks around.

GREGORY
Lighter?

JENNY
Hmmm. I don't know. Probably in my purse.

GREGORY
Where is that?

JENNY
Not sure about that either. Oh. Over there.

He hands it to her. She takes a hit.

GREGORY
How is it?

JENNY
Good. Very good. So I'm thinking of getting the house painted.

GREGORY
Really?

JENNY
Yeah. Why not?

GREGORY
Money?

JENNY
I'm setting up a reverse mortgage to pay for the nursing services. And a bathroom downstairs. It might be time to update the painting. Do you know what color you'd want your room to be?

GREGORY
Something not pink.

JENNY
That room was last painted when it was my room 50 years ago.

GREGORY
What about Lynn?

JENNY
She didn't object.

GREGORY
Ga seems okay. I mean, you thought she was going to die and she didn't.

JENNY
She's almost 92, honey. She can't walk anymore. Her breathing is awful. She's on oxygen all the time.

GREGORY
Except when she's smoking. And her nurse signed off on that.

JENNY
Don't bag on Debbie. I like her, a lot. You see how bad the weekend nurses are. I don't think I'm going to keep using them.

GREGORY
Really?

JENNY
It doesn't make sense to pay for someone to come in on the weekends when they're terrible and don't care. I think for two days a week, I can do it myself. We can do it.

GREGORY
I don't know. Is that thing cashed? *(JENNY has been holding the pipe. She passes it back. He tries it.)* Yeah. Here, where's the bag?

JENNY
Oh. Here.

GREGORY
I just found the last year to be overwhelming. I still do. It's just ... I was on my own much of the last few years. It was fine at first. She didn't ... she wasn't ... you know. And then, I didn't really know how to handle it.

JENNY
You handled it fine.

GREGORY
No, I didn't. She got sick. And I didn't even notice. I was so happy and excited to get out of here, to have the burden off of me, I didn't even notice she wasn't feeling well.

JENNY
You did, too. You told me she wasn't feeling well.

GREGORY
I told you she had a cold. Not that she might be dying.

JENNY
How could you know that?

GREGORY
I should have known!

JENNY
How?

GREGORY
She almost died! You said you thought she was going to die!

JENNY
It looked that way, honey, but she didn't.

GREGORY
But she is, isn't she?

JENNY
There's no telling how long she has, but she isn't going to get better. She's lived a good long life, Gregory. And we're making her comfortable. Ultimately that's why we both came here.(Beat) Are you okay?

GREGORY
I don't know. I mean, yeah, I'll be okay. I'm going to get ready for bed.

JENNY
Okay, and Greg?

GREGORY
Yeah?

JENNY
Can you do me a favor? Can you move all your painting stuff?

GREGORY
That's where I like to paint.

JENNY
I know but/

GREGORY
That's how I/

JENNY
I know, but we've cleaned up the rest of the room.

GREGORY
I know, it's like a hospital room in there.

JENNY
But it isn't a hospital room, and it isn't a room at a home. It's her own house. I'm just asking you to clean up a little.

GREGORY
I've cleaned up a lot. I've done the best I could.

JENNY
Oh, Gregory, I'm not/

GREGORY
I had a lot of the burden, most of the burden, these years.

JENNY
I know, and I'm sorry about that.

GREGORY
And I'm glad to have the help. I'm glad to not have to make decisions for her that are life and death. But that doesn't mean I want to be erased from her entire life.

JENNY
I'm not saying that, Gregory.

GREGORY
It feels that way.

JENNY

I'm sorry it feels that way to you. It's just taking up the entire bay window, and Debbie could use that area.

GREGORY

Debbie could.

JENNY

Yes. Ga's nurse. For Ga's clothes and medicines.

LALA sleeps. GREGORY enters, stacks paintings, packs his easel. It snaps closed.

LALA

Oh, it's you, darling.

GREGORY

Hi, honey; it's me.

LALA

I thought you were grandfather. No one knows what happened to him. During the revolution, I mean. He was fleeing to Poland. He was Polish by birth, and many of his estates were there.

GREGORY

I didn't know he was Polish. What happened to him?

LALA

No one knows. We never heard from him again. My mother thinks his nurse stabbed him in the back and took his money.

GREGORY

Why did she think that?

LALA

I don't know. It was a confusing time. I was a little girl and I had the Spanish flu. I almost died myself. What are you doing, darling?

GREGORY

Packing up my painting stuff.

LALA

Oh, Gregory! Why?

GREGORY

Mom says Debbie needs space for your medicines and clothes.

LALA

It's not a normal thing, for your daughter to be taking care of you. Before that, you were here, but it was more like we were taking care of each other.

GREGORY

Yeah. That was nice.

LALA
I agree. (Beat) I wish you would leave that one painting.

GREGORY
You do?

LALA
Yes, I like your paintings. Why do you say it like that?

GREGORY
Mom says my paintings are dark.

LALA
I like them. And I just want to have a couple of them back.

GREGORY
You'll have to talk to Mom about that.

LALA
I will. She's still my daughter.

GREGORY
Which ones?

LALA
What darling?

GREGORY
Which paintings do you like?

LALA
I don't know.

GREGORY
I knew it was too good to be true.

LALA
I think there was one landscape, like outside of our house, with the river and the trees through our stone archway.

GREGORY
You do remember?

LALA
Yes. And then there was one. I don't know what it was exactly. Like symbols. But it had my initials. L-E.

GREGORY
Yes. There was one like that.

LALA
I don't know what it was I liked, but it spoke to me. Maybe you could just bring that one back.

GREGORY
Sure. If Mom says it's okay.

LALA
You leave your mother to me.

He kisses her cheek, moves downstage.

GREGORY

She was the one who saw her initials in the painting. I didn't paint it that way. I painted the Chinese symbol for death. Freaked me out that she saw it, but I looked and there it was. I never thought about her dying. Not when I moved here and not for many years. I think, with an older relative, you take for granted they'll be there forever. Hell, when you're a kid, you don't really understand age anyway. You just know your grandparents are old. So by the time you're an adult, they've been old forever. I knew she needed help. That she had fallen a few times, had trouble with tenants, whatever. I needed some help, too. I was working in this small, suffocating Southern town, writing for a newspaper, being disliked by unlikable people. Not meeting anyone. People judging me based on ... whatever. I couldn't take it anymore, the depression and the isolation, and my Mom said my grandmother needed someone ... needed me. And I needed her, too. It's weird, but I look back on the awful things that led me here ... Now I think of them as blessings.

Act THREE, Scene TWO

Afternoon. LALA sleeps. DEBBIE cleans the kitchen. JENNY enters, with bags.

DEBBIE
Jenny. I didn't think you were coming back so soon.

JENNY
I think if I haven't left by now ...

DEBBIE
Do you need any help with that?

JENNY
I've got this. There's big stuff in the car. Is Gregory here?

DEBBIE
No. I think he went down to the city.

JENNY
Oh. That's good, too.

DEBBIE
Jenny, you're funny.

JENNY
I know. I'm a bad mother.

DEBBIE
That's not true. I wish my son would smoke pot with me.

JENNY
You do?

DEBBIE
Instead of doing who the knows what, with who knows who, who know where in the Bronx? Yeah!

JENNY
Speaking of enabling, I have more vodka, and for us, mudslides, courtesy of TGIF. They make pre-made mudslides. How does that sound?

DEBBIE
Oh, Jenny, you know how that sounds? Gooo-oood.

JENNY
Great. How do you drink them?

DEBBIE
You know, one and then another.

JENNY
I mean, with milk, or over ice?

DEBBIE
Ice is good.

JENNY gets ice and DEBBIE pours.

JENNY
Do you want to sit at the table or go into the other room?

DEBBIE
I don't mind sitting in here. Lala is resting so well today, it would be a shame to wake her. Should we toast?

JENNY
Sure. What shall we toast to?

DEBBIE
How about, to strong women?

JENNY
That sounds good. A toast to strong women.

DEBBIE
I don't know about you, but I don't need no man in my life. I've found they are nothing but trouble.

JENNY
Do you mean black men?

DEBBIE
Black men, brown men, white men, purple men, striped men, polka dot men. Any man.

JENNY
A-men.

DEBBIE
Girl, I bet if they find life on Mars, within a few years, we'll learn their women are decent folk

and the men are lyin, cheatin, warrin dirtbags. What about you? You done?

JENNY

I don't know.

DEBBIE

Dating a black man wasn't enough for you?

JENNY

Well, he was enough, for sure. But he was somewhat feral.

DEBBIE

That's their natural state.

JENNY

He had substance abuse issues. He was practically homeless when I met him.

DEBBIE

And where is he now?

JENNY

Pretty much homeless.

DEBBIE

Ashes to ashes, dust to dust. You miss him?

JENNY

I don't miss being hit.

DEBBIE
Oh, Jenny. I didn't know.

JENNY
No. No one did. I didn't even know until it was too late. Mother knew. In some odd way, I think she knows.

DEBBIE
She's a smart one.

JENNY
Drives me crazy.

DEBBIE
Your momma always knows. So, no more men for me.

JENNY
What about your son?

DEBBIE
Oh Jenny, he's out in the world, too. But I've got Christine, my daughter. She's a good one. Of course, she's dating.

JENNY laughs. Then they both laugh.

LALA
I'm glad to hear something is so funny in there. Meanwhile I'm all alone and need some help in here.

They take their drinks and go into the other room. LALA is awake and agitated.

JENNY

Hi, mom.

DEBBIE

Lala, how are you?

LALA

I'm good. But I'm thirsty, and I think I wet the bed.

DEBBIE checks. She springs into action.

DEBBIE

You sure did. But it's no problem.

LALA

That's easy for you to say. And I really am thirsty.

JENNY

I'll get you something, Mom. Do you need water?

LALA

Maybe with some coffee?

JENNY

I'll get it.

JENNY exits. DEBBIE is a whirlwind, changing and cleaning.

LALA
Fancy meeting you here.

DEBBIE
It's okay, Lala. It's what happens when you stop walking.

LALA
I didn't mean to stop.

DEBBIE
After you got sick, you refused physical therapy.

LALA
I was too old to work like that. I'm almost 92. Or 93. My immigration papers made me a year younger because my mother wanted to be younger. But either way, that's pretty old.

DEBBIE
You still could have tried to walk again Lala.

LALA
Well, I didn't. Is it too late now?

DEBBIE
Lala, do you want to do some therapy?

LALA
I'd rather just have a drink and a ciggie. Can I?

DEBBIE
It's okay, Lala. We were just having a drink ourselves.

LALA
Oh, sure. You guys were having a party without me.

DEBBIE
You can join us, Lala. Or we can join you.

JENNY enters with coffee and a pastry.

LALA
Oh, thank you. But we were discussing vodka and ciggies.

JENNY
Oh, were you?

LALA
Cigaretta, cigaretta.

JENNY
Oh, mother.

DEBBIE
It's okay, I'll turn off the oxygen, and we'll all sit in here and drink and smoke.

LALA
Oh, Debbie, you're the best nurse ever.

DEBBIE
Thanks, Lala.

DEBBIE turns off the oxygen.

JENNY
Mother, we're having mudslides. Do you want one?

LALA
A what?

DEBBIE
You didn't have mudslides in Russia, Lala? It has vodka.

LALA finds a coffee cup, holds it out.

JENNY
I'll get it.

DEBBIE
I got it, Jenny. Give the woman her smoke.

LALA
I second that!

JENNY lights up two cigarettes, gives her mother one. DEBBIE gets up and goes to the kitchen to make another drink.

LALA
Oh, that's nice. So Jenny, I wanted to talk to you about something. I was wondering about all my stuff.

JENNY
What stuff, mother?

LALA
Well, I had a table here, a couch. Lots of stuff.

JENNY
The couch is right here, mom. It's just over here against this window rather than that window.

LALA
Oh, it looks different from here. What about the other stuff?

JENNY
I'm not sure what other stuff you mean.

LALA
I don't know. What did I used to have on my table?

JENNY
What didn't you have? Checks, bills, magazines, cigs, matches, lighters, ashtrays, shot glasses, glasses, ointments.

LALA
Yes. And where is all of that?

JENNY
Some has been cleaned up, put back at the desk, for instance.

LALA
Irving's desk?

JENNY
Yes. Some of it, like cigs and matches and lighters, I have.

LALA
I wish I didn't have to wait for special occasions for them.

JENNY
Yes, well, you are currently smoking a cigarette. Or not smoking it, as the case may be. Here mother, why don't you ash into the ashtray and not on the bed.

LALA
Yes. Thank you darling. But I wanted to ask something.

JENNY
What?

LALA
I ... you know, I don't remember. Oh. Yes. There used to be paintings around here.

JENNY
Yes. Gregory's stuff.

LALA
Yes. Painting things.

JENNY
Lots of stuff.

LALA
But some of the paintings. The windows aren't so great but I liked to see his paintings.

JENNY
I find them to be kind of dark.

LALA
Well, maybe I liked them dark.

JENNY
We just cleaned up the bay window so we could put some clothes and medicines there.

LALA
Well, there was one I liked.

JENNY
Which one?

LALA
I don't know.

JENNY
Well, let me track it right down for you then.

LALA
I think it had my initials on it. I don't know what it was exactly. Gregory said it was a symbol. But I don't what it was a symbol of, only that it looked like an L and an E.

JENNY
Okay. I'll talk to him about it.

LALA
And Jenny, there's something else. Don't say anything to Gregory.

JENNY
Why wouldn't I tell him you like his painting?

LALA
No. I mean, you know.

JENNY
I won't tell him if you tell me what not to tell him.

LALA
You know. That I'm not getting any better.

JENNY
Oh, mother, that's not for any of us to say.

LALA
Oh, come on. I know. I used to dance. Then I didn't dance anymore. Now I can't move at all.

JENNY
You always were one for the dramatic, mother. I wonder where Gregory gets it from.

LALA
Irving was into the arts. He reminds me of Irving a little.

JENNY
I don't know.

LALA
Not a lot. But in some of the things he says. Like how he calls me honey.

JENNY
For different reasons.

LALA
Or, I don't know, once he arrived, I felt something.

JENNY
Like what?

LALA
I don't know. Secure. Less nervous. And sometimes, happy.

DEBBIE returns with LALA's drink. She finds her own stuff, settles in.

LALA
Ah, thank you Debbie.

DEBBIE
You're welcome, but Jenny bought it.

LALA
Thank you, too. This is good. What did you call it again?

DEBBIE
A mudslide.

LALA
A mudslide. Very good. You know, vodka is from Russia, too.

JENNY
Mother, Debbie was asking about your dancing career.

DEBBIE
Lala, how old were you when you started?

LALA

Eight. Or maybe nine. It's hard to know. When we got to America, my mother made me younger, so she could be younger.

DEBBIE

She did not!

LALA

She did!

DEBBIE

I wish I'd though of that! What was Russia like Lala?

LALA

I liked being a little girl in Russia. In summer, we would go on vacation. I remember going to grandfather's estates, and it was always a big game, which one we would visit.

DEBBIE

Estates?

LALA

Yes. He had so many, we never knew where we would vacation.

DEBBIE

I'd settle for one estate. What happened to them?

LALA
I don't know. After the revolution, grandfather disappeared. We heard his nurse killed him and took his money.

JENNY
It was just a rumor. Maybe the communists got him.

LALA
He was Polish. He should have been allowed to leave. My father was from Ukraine. That's why he was let out of jail.

DEBBIE
He was in jail?

LALA
Oh sure, during the Revolution. But he escaped.

DEBBIE
I thought he was let out?

LALA
Oh yes, he was. I'm getting confused. The first time they let him out, if he would go home. Of course, we lived in Petrograd. St. Petersburg. Not Ukraine. So they captured him again. Then he escaped.

DEBBIE
And he went back there?

LALA
Not to Petrograd. He did go to Ukraine. Grandfather had an estate in Crimea, too, but we had left there and gone to Turkey. So he followed us and found us in Turkey.

DEBBIE
He did not!

LALA
Oh, yes, he did.

DEBBIE
Jenny, you knew this?

JENNY
All my life. If it wasn't mom telling us, it was Bobbi, my grandmother.

DEBBIE
Oh, man. It makes life in the Bronx seem tame.

LALA
You live in the Bronx?

JENNY
Debbie lives near the hospital where Jeff did his residency. She lives a few blocks away from where we used to live.

DEBBIE
You used to live in the Bronx, too, Lala?

LALA
Not me. I grew up in Manhattan. I mean, after we got here.

DEBBIE
When was that?

LALA
When I was 12. Or 13. It's hard to tell because mother changed my age. Did I tell you that?

DEBBIE
Yes, Lala, you did.

LALA
When we got here we lived on the West Side, where there were a lot of Russians. It seemed like everyone we knew from Petrograd and from Turkey had come to New York.

DEBBIE
Were you scared? Wandering around a new city?

LALA
I guess I was at first. But having so many friends and family here made it seem like home.

JENNY
And the libraries, mother.

LALA

What about them?

JENNY

I remember you saying you felt at home when you found the library.

LALA

Oh, yes. They had a Russian section in the New York public library. So, I could learn English. I knew Russian and French, and that was enough to get around.

DEBBIE

You must have been good in school.

LALA

No. I mean, I liked it, but at 12, they put me in first grade because of the language. Then third, then fifth. By then I was 15 and dancing full time. So I dropped out. The thing is, we were in New York City, in the midst of a real boom. And I had access to books, and later records and radio. I learned. And they had amazing culture here. I guess they still do. I can't remember the last time I went down to the city.

JENNY

Your 90th birthday, with Lynn to the Music Hall reunion.

LALA

Radio City?

JENNY

Yes. They had hundreds of old dancers, Rockettes, stage hands, for a reunion, and they all sang "Happy Birthday" to mother.

DEBBIE

Oh, how nice!

JENNY

It sounded like it was nice. Of course, Lynn got to go.

DEBBIE

What? You didn't get to go?

JENNY

Lynn worked there when she was younger.

DEBBIE

You didn't, Jenny?

JENNY

No. My dad had died by the time I was old enough to work.

LALA

He was a stage manager, you see. And he could have had his pick of any of the girls there.

DEBBIE
Who, Lala? Your husband?

LALA
Yes. I mean, the Rockette girls, the other ballerinas, the singers, anyone. I could hear the other girls talk about him. They couldn't believe it when he was interested in me.

DEBBIE
I can believe he was, Lala.

LALA
I couldn't. Sometimes I look back and I still don't.

JENNY
I think mother was different than the other woman there.

LALA
I'll say.

Everyone laughs. Drinks.

Act THREE, Scene THREE

Weeks later. Middle of the night.

LALA
I used to be a dancer. Did I say that already? Father found a job training horses. Actually, what he did was teach girls from wealthy

families to ride. Sometimes he had to train the horses first. He said in America, only the girls wanted to learn to ride horses. But ... I always wondered why he wasn't as interested in my dancing. I mean, he liked it. But it wasn't the same as when he was watching a student ride. He was a horseman. He liked horses. He liked people who could ride horses. He didn't even seem to acknowledge when it was my dancing that paid our bills. That paid our passage to America. I guess it must have been hard for him, like it was for grandfather when I would take his money at cards.

GREGORY comes down in night clothes.

GREGORY
Ga, is that you?

LALA
Yes. No one here but us witches.

GREGORY
Who were you talking to?

LALA
Oh. I don't know, actually. Irving, maybe. Possibly father.

GREGORY
What were you talking to them about?

LALA
Um, you know, I don't remember. Must not have been too important. Can I ask you a question?

GREGORY
Yes.

LALA
Is somebody coming?

GREGORY
Yes. Lynn, and perhaps some of her kids.

LALA
Oh.

GREGORY
What oh? You like seeing Lynn.

LALA
It's not that.

GREGORY
The kids?

LALA
Is there anything to drink?

GREGORY
Like some water or something?

LALA
I was thinking maybe vodka.

GREGORY
I don't know if we have any.

LALA
I am sort of thirsty.

GREGORY
I'm pretty sure we have some ginger ale. I'll get you some.

LALA
Oh, that would be nice. One summer grandfather taught me to play poker. He thought it would be nice to have someone to beat. But then I won! He said it was beginner's luck, but I won again. He got so angry, he stopped playing with me. He told mother it reflected poorly on her that she'd raise a child with such bad manners as to beat her elders at poker.

GREGORY returns with a glass.

GREGORY
Here you go.

LALA
Oh, that's nice. Is that the purple ginger ale you buy?

GREGORY
It's grape. I'm glad you like it.

LALA
It's good. You know what would go great with it? Some vodka.

GREGORY
Somehow I thought you'd say that.

LALA
I'm just saying it would add a nice flavor to it. I don't know if I even have any vodka. I'll have to call that man. I forget his name. At the liquor store. Sometimes they deliver. Sometimes they don't. It used to be when they couldn't deliver to me, I would drive there and just honk my horn, and they would bring it out for me. I don't know what happened to my car. Do I still have a car?

GREGORY
No.

LALA
Do you know what happened to it?

GREGORY
Yes. It stopped working.

LALA
I bet they could have fixed it.

GREGORY
Maybe they could have.

LALA
What I don't understand is who decided to get rid of it.

GREGORY
I'm sorry, honey, I did. You hadn't driven it in more than a year, and when I drove it, it broke down on me. It needed a new engine, and the guy at the garage said it would cost thousands to fix.

LALA
My guy at the garage? He said that?

GREGORY
Yes. Maybe I made the wrong decision. I'm sorry if I did.

LALA
It's not really fair. I have two daughters and one house, and it is split between the two of them. So there's nothing for you, and it makes me feel bad.

GREGORY
It shouldn't. You've given me more than enough.

LALA
How?

GREGORY
Just giving me a place to land. That was what I needed.

LALA
But what about when I'm gone?

GREGORY
I don't know. I'll be okay.

LALA
I know you will. I just want you to have something. I want you to get married and have a family and provide for them.

GREGORY
Me, too.

LALA
It's just I wanted you to have my car.

GREGORY
Oh, honey. That's sweet.

LALA
And now I have nothing to give you.

GREGORY
That's not true. You've done so much for me. Besides, I have my truck. And if I move into the city, I won't need a car.

LALA
It would be nice if you could stay here.

GREGORY
I wish I could, but I don't know how Mom and Aunt Lynn feel.

LALA
You could ask them.

GREGORY
I could. But it's their decision to make, and they'll make it when the time is right. I don't think what I want matters.

LALA
They've been waiting a long time for this.

GREGORY
Don't say it that way.

LALA
No, but ... Is somebody coming next week?

GREGORY
Yes. Lynn and her kids.

LALA
All of them?

GREGORY
No. Some of them.

LALA
Because I don't have a place to put them all.

GREGORY
I think they'll stay in a hotel.

LALA
And now they're coming to bury me.

GREGORY
They're coming to say goodbye.

LALA
Same thing. I took Lisa to look at colleges. Did you know?

GREGORY
Yes.

LALA
And she doesn't even visit.

GREGORY
She lives in Seattle.

LALA
Where?

GREGORY
Seattle. Washington state.

LALA
Oh. Is she coming on this trip?

GREGORY
No. She has like five kids. And lives 3,000 miles away.

LALA
I'd just like to see her.

GREGORY
Look at it this way, I probably haven't seen her in 20 years.

LALA
I meant to tell you, thank you for bringing back my painting.

GREGORY
You're welcome.

LALA
I know some people think it's dark. But I like it.

GREGORY
I prefer to think of it as colorful.

LALA
That's a good way of looking at it.

GREGORY
I think so.

LALA
Do you know who this woman is?

GREGORY

What woman?

LALA

There's this woman, I guess she is living here now.

GREGORY

One of the tenants?

LALA

I don't think so. She says she's Jenny.

GREGORY

You mean Mom?

LALA

I don't know. It's just very strange. Is it Lily?

GREGORY

Who is Lily?

LALA

A girl who danced with me after I arrived in America. And I can't figure out what she's doing back here with us.

GREGORY

Lily?

LALA

Well. This woman.

GREGORY

Jenny?

LALA

If you say so.

GREGORY

I say so.

LALA

Oh, darling. It's good you came home.

Act THREE, Scene FOUR

Daytime. LALA sleeps. DEBBIE cleans. LYNN enters with grocery bags.

DEBBIE

Here, Lynn, let me help you with that.

LYNN

Thank you. I don't know where everyone else is.

DEBBIE

Gregory is at work. Jenny is in Maryland.

LYNN

Maryland? She didn't want to see her sister?

DEBBIE

She does. She said she hopes to be back before you leave.

LYNN
I have to leave Sunday.

DEBBIE
She had a trial. She'll be back late Friday, or maybe Saturday, depending on what time court gets out.

LYNN
She'll miss her nephews.

DEBBIE
Are they here? I guess I haven't met them yet.

LYNN
They came in late last night. They've got some stuff to do today, but they'll be by later to say hello.

DEBBIE
Did they stay here?

LYNN
With Jenny in one room and Gregory in another, there is hardly room for me. They're at a hotel. You would think she'd want to see them.

DEBBIE
I think she wants to do her work and not miss a court date. She said she's looking forward to seeing her sister.

LYNN
I'm looking forward to seeing her. It looks nice in here.

DEBBIE
Thank you.

LYNN
It's clean like a kitchen is supposed to be. It's great. It is cleaner here than it has been in 40 years.

DEBBIE
You exaggerate.

LYNN
I don't. Mother had a green thumb, and she was a wonderful dancer, I guess, but she wasn't a cleaner. And my grandmother, Bobbi, she was more of a socialite.

DEBBIE
I've heard that.

LYNN
It's not your job. Most caretakers don't. Won't.

DEBBIE
Well, I look at it this way. I'm here. Maybe I could sit around and watch television all day. But if I do that, I ignore my job. So I might as well do some chores to pass the time. I like to

have a clean work place. And your mom isn't any trouble. I have a lot of extra time.

LYNN
She's been trouble my entire life. Probably her entire life.

DEBBIE
Oh, Lynn. You shouldn't say things like that.

LYNN
It's my experience. The smoking. The drinking. The inability to listen to anything anyone has to say. That I have to say.

DEBBIE
Mommas are like that. I'm sure my kids think that about me.

LYNN
You have kids?

DEBBIE
Two. A boy and a girl.

LYNN
I'm sure they don't think that about you.

DEBBIE
You think yours don't think that about you?

LYNN
No. I know they do. Or I suspect they do.

DEBBIE
Then how do you deal with it?

LYNN
I drink a lot of coffee, and I focus on the tasks at hand. I have a lot to do.

DEBBIE
Did you mean in general or a lot to do right now?

LYNN
Both. I'm making pashka.

DEBBIE
Who?

LYNN
Pashka.

DEBBIE
Is that some crazy white folks food?

LYNN
No, it's ... well, yes. I guess it is. Crazy Russian anyway. It's a tradition that will die with me.

DEBBIE
Why's that?

LYNN
In our family no one else knows how to make it. Not even Jenny.

DEBBIE
What about your kids?

LYNN
Not the boys. I think their wives do the cooking. I tried to show Lisa, my daughter, but she didn't like it.

DEBBIE
Too much work?

LYNN
No. I mean, yes, but she didn't like eating it. She wasn't interested in cooking something that took all day and no one wanted to eat. Bobbi showed me how to make this. And the meat and eggplant pies mother likes. I used to make them when I was a girl. I'm not sure father liked them, but he ate every bite. He was ... he was good. My youngest child reminds me of him. Bren. He's good to me. Mom said Bobbi wasn't good at anything, but Bobbi taught me Russian. She taught me how to cook. I think she was good at a few things. You know, Jenny was the favorite, and then Gregory. I don't know why. I don't know what causes you to treat your children differently. Except I do it with Bren, too.

DEBBIE
I don't know.

LYNN
Do you have a difficult relationship with your daughter?

DEBBIE
No. My son.

LYNN
Why?

DEBBIE
I'm a single mom. He's a teenage boy in the Bronx. It's hard. I know that.

LYNN
My kids went to private school in San Antonio, and it was still hard.

DEBBIE
Oh, Lynn, it's just life.

LYNN
I like work. I can control work. I work hard, go on the road, train our clients and make my reports.

DEBBIE
I understand. I get a new client. I cook. I clean. I change. I feed. I follow the directions on the medicines.

LYNN
That would be hard for some people.

DEBBIE
Some people get along with their daughters, some people get along with their son.

LYNN
And some people don't get along with their mothers.

Act THREE, Scene FIVE

Late. LALA is awake, watching TV. JENNY enters from the front, with a suitcase.

LALA
Oh, it's you.

JENNY
Yes, mother, it's me.

LALA
Where did you come from?

JENNY
Well, I was in Maryland, but now I'm home.

LALA
Well, it's so nice of you to come over and see me. Have you seen either of my daughters?

JENNY

Yes. I'm pretty sure I've seen Jenny, and Lynn is around somewhere. Maybe asleep.

LALA

And who are you?

JENNY

I'm your daughter, Jenny.

LALA

Oh. I thought you were Lily.

JENNY

Yes. I know.

LALA

Did you have a nice trip, all the way from Europe?

JENNY

Something like that.

LALA

Listen, Lily, can I ask you something? Can you get me something to drink?

JENNY

Of course, mother. What would you like?

LALA

Some tea, maybe. If it isn't too much trouble.

JENNY
It isn't any trouble. Would you like it with lemon and sugar?

LALA
I don't want to bother you.

JENNY
It's no bother. I was going to make you tea anyway.

LALA
Oh, Lily. You always were a fresh one.

JENNY goes to the kitchen. LYNN enters.

LYNN
Hello, stranger.

JENNY
Hi. You didn't have to get up on my account.

They embrace somewhat stiffly.

LYNN
I got up on account of a cigarette and a glass of water. There's meat and eggplant pies. And pashka tomorrow.

JENNY
I thought I saw signs of pashka. That's wonderful.

LYNN
You almost missed me. I have to leave tomorrow afternoon.

JENNY
I wanted to leave this morning, but I had a list of chores.

LYNN
Mother up?

JENNY
She was. I'm making her the tea she asked for.

LYNN
You missed the boys.

JENNY
I'm sorry to hear that. All three?

LYNN
No. I didn't bring Bren. He's too young to see this.

JENNY
I thought he was 16?

LYNN
All those years, we said she was never going to go.

JENNY
It's not too late, you know?

LYNN
What's not too late?

JENNY
You know. To have a conversation with her.

LYNN
I have conversations with her.

JENNY
You know what I mean. Clear the air. Whatever bad feelings you've had for the last 50 years.

LYNN
What bad feelings?

JENNY
Oh, don't bullshit, Lynn.

LYNN
I'm not bullshitting. I just think mother liked you best.

JENNY
I know.

LYNN
And after father died, when I needed her most, do you know where she was?

JENNY
Sitting alone in that room with a bottle of vodka.

LYNN
Yes.

JENNY
And where were you when I needed you? When we did?

LYNN
I was going to school.

JENNY
You could have stayed. You didn't have to go early.

LYNN
I did. I didn't want to stay and watch her.

JENNY
I had to stay here and watch. And the one person who might have helped me just ran off to school.

LYNN
I had to. There was no way I wasn't going.

JENNY
Well, it sure didn't make life easy on me.

LYNN
You should have said something.

JENNY
Would it have made a difference?

LYNN
No, but it would be better than letting it fester.

JENNY
I didn't have the capacity then. But I did say something now.

LYNN
Yes, so?

JENNY
It feels better.

LYNN
Good.

JENNY
Then why can't you do the same thing with mother?

LYNN
If I do, will you stop?

JENNY
Stop what?

LYNN
Telling me what I should do.

JENNY
I'm not telling you anything. I'm talking to you about your issues with mother that you've had all of your adult life.

LYNN
And telling me what to do about them.

JENNY
If that's what you think, I guess I'm okay with that. Here.

LYNN
What's this?

JENNY
Mother's tea.

LYNN
For what?

JENNY
I made her some tea to drink. Why don't you go take it to her and have a little talk with her.

LYNN
You mean now?

JENNY
No time like the present. Here you go.

LYNN

What?

JENNY

The tea!

LYNN

Oh. Yes.

JENNY

Remember it doesn't have to be any big thing.

LYNN

It doesn't?

JENNY

No. Just have a talk with mother. While there's still time.

LYNN takes the tea and cigarettes. JENNY sits. LYNN enters living room.

LALA

Jenny?

LYNN

No, mother, it's Lynn.

LALA

Oh, Lynn. It's so nice to see you.

LYNN
It's nice to see you, too.

LALA
When did you get here?

LYNN
Three days ago.

LALA
Oh. Wow. Did I see you?

LYNN
Yes. And the boys.

LALA
What are their names again?

LYNN
Scooter and Christopher.

LALA
Oh, yes. That's a very strange name. Scooter.

LYNN
His real name is Joseph.

LALA
Like your husband?

LYNN
Ex-husband.

LALA
And they were here? Did I see them?

LYNN
Yes, mother.

LALA
Is Gregory here?

LYNN
Yes.

LALA
Where is he?

LYNN
I'm guessing asleep.

LALA
Sleeping in, is he?

LYNN
No mother, it's one in the morning.

LALA
Oh. I lose track of time.

LYNN
I know.

LALA
Well, you mustn't get mad at me darling. My head isn't always working right.

LYNN
I know. Here's your tea.

LALA
Oh, thank you. You're so good to me.

LYNN gets up to leave.

LALA
Lynn?

LYNN
Yes?

LALA
Thank you for the tea.

LYNN
You're welcome, mother. I need to get to bed.

LALA
You do?

LYNN
Yes, it's late and I have to leave tomorrow.

LALA
Oh. What time is it now?

LYNN
One.

LALA

In the morning?

LYNN

Yes.

LALA

Oh. You'd better get to bed then.

LYNN

Yes. Good night.

LALA

Good night, darling.

LYNN lingers, in indecision. Then she leaves and quickly exits up the stairs. JENNY enters. She has been listening.

JENNY

Hi, mom.

LALA

Oh, Jenny. It's so good to see you. When did you get home?

JENNY

About an hour ago.

LALA

Oh, it's so nice to have you home. Have you seen your sister?

JENNY
Yes.

LALA
I'm glad you got to see her before she left. I worry about her. She works too hard.

JENNY
Did you guys talk about anything?

LALA
Like what?

JENNY
Just life. You guys. Her childhood. Anything.

LALA
No. But she had a good childhood. I don't know why we would talk about that.

JENNY
I don't know. The important thing is she loves you and you love her. Right?

LALA
Of course I love her. How could I not love my own daughter?

JENNY
I know. I'm glad we've had our talks.

LALA
Oh, Jenny, so am I.

JENNY
I wish Lynn could have had the same.

LALA
Oh, Lynn? Is she here?

Act THREE, Scene SIX

GREGORY is with LALA. DEBBIE is in the kitchen with JENNY.

JENNY
I wish I knew what it was.

DEBBIE
Does it bother you?

JENNY
I don't know. I mean, it did at first. How could my own mother not recognize me? But whomever she thinks I am, she seems to enjoy my company. And she accepts my help. So if I get past the ego thing, what does it matter?

DEBBIE
I've seen this a lot, Jenny. She's traveling.

JENNY
Traveling?

DEBBIE
Yes. In and out of this life. Getting ready for the next. She's clearly working some stuff out. Stuff with her parents. Stuff with you girls. Stuff with her husband.

JENNY
Wow. I'm sorry she has so much stuff to work out.

DEBBIE
Don't we all? I think it is peaceful. Or natural anyway.

JENNY
I hope so.

DEBBIE
I've seen worse. I've had folks where the kids never show up to say goodbye. Where the kids never show up to help. Or take it out on a parent, controlling, being mean, blaming.

JENNY
As if any of us can help it.

DEBBIE
Jenny, it will come for us some day, too.

Light up on the living room.

LALA
What does it look like?

GREGORY
Oh, it looks nice, you know.

LALA
No. I don't know. That's why I am asking.

GREGORY
Like it did before, only now all the rooms are painted.

LALA
That sounds different.

GREGORY
Well, it's pretty much the same, but clean and nice.

LALA
So it wasn't nice before?

GREGORY
It was nice before. Just old and run down.

LALA
Like me.

GREGORY
Well then let's get you a new coat of paint.

LALA
Oh, very funny. I wish I could see it.

GREGORY
I bet you can.

LALA
How?

GREGORY
I can carry you up.

LALA
Upstairs?

GREGORY
Why not?

LALA
I don't know if they'll let me.

GREGORY
Who?

LALA
Jenny or Debbie or Lily.

GREGORY
Who?

LALA
You mother and my nurse. And the lady that's here at night.

GREGORY
Let's ask them.

LALA
Right now? Do you think they will?

GREGORY
Why not?

LALA
Why not! Where are they?

GREGORY
The kitchen.

LALA
Jen-ny. Deb-bie.

JENNY and DEBBIE enter.

JENNY
Hi, mom.

LALA
Gregory and I were wondering, if, well, how should I put it? Gregory, help me out here

GREGORY
Ga would like to see the upstairs.

LALA
I was wondering what it looks like. Would I be allowed to see?

JENNY
Yes, of course. I've been wanting you to see. I just don't know how to get you up there.

GREGORY
I'll carry her up.

JENNY
You'll just have to be careful.

GREGORY
I will.

LALA
I just need to be freed here.

DEBBIE
I'll unhook you, Lala.

DEBBIE begins to unhook LALA from the oxygen. Jenny brings her the wheelchair.

LALA
Thank you. Since we're turning off the oxygen, maybe I can have a ciggie when we're done.

JENNY
One thing at a time.

DEBBIE
Here, get Lala in the chair. I'll wheel you to the steps.

They do. DEBBIE wheels her over.

JENNY
Now how are we going to do this?

GREGORY
I was just going to carry her up in my arms.

JENNY
My goodness. What if you fall?

GREGORY
I won't.

DEBBIE
How about on your back? Like piggy back.

JENNY
That might work.

GREGORY
Here, let's try. Here, Ga, grab my neck.

DEBBIE
I'll take the wheelchair up so we can wheel you around.

DEBBIE hurries by.

JENNY
Take your time. If you can't do it, don't take the risk.

GREGORY
We can do it. Here we go.

JENNY follows, as if guarding an egg.

JENNY
Be careful.

GREGORY
I am.

LALA
Go slow, darling.

GREGORY
I am.

DEBBIE
How is it, Lala?

LALA
I'm fine.

GREGORY
Look, here we are.

GREGORY puts LALA in the wheelchair.

LALA
Wow.

GREGORY
What do you think?

JENNY

It's nice, huh?

LALA

It's very nice. Did you do all of this?

JENNY

Well, the workmen, remember?

LALA

No, but they did an amazing job. This one is a funny color.

JENNY

It's purple.

LALA

Is this where you're sleeping? It isn't what I would have picked.

JENNY

I know.

DEBBIE

I like it, Lala. It's different.

LALA

Gregory?

GREGORY

Yes?

LALA
What do you think?

GREGORY
I like it. But it is even better in my room.

LALA
Oh, I haven't seen that one yet.

DEBBIE
Here, we'll go that way.

JENNY
This used to be my room, Debbie, when I was a girl.

DEBBIE
Oh, I didn't know that.

GREGORY
And it was pink.

LALA
Not fit for a young man.

GREGORY
Peeling pink at that. Peeling pink paint.

LALA
Oh, it's so blue.

GREGORY
So blue!

LALA
Well, Jenny, you did a very nice job.

JENNY
Thanks, Mom.

LALA
Thank you. For everything.

GREGORY
Here, are you ready to go back down?

LALA
I guess so.

GREGORY
Here, let's get back on.

LALA
I will. Go slow down the stairs.

GREGORY
I will.

The two of them go downstairs. JENNY and DEBBIE stay behind.

JENNY
It really does look nice, doesn't it?

DEBBIE
Yes, Jenny. It really does look nice.

JENNY
It was in such disrepair all these years.

DEBBIE
It's a beautiful house. You did a good job, Jenny. It looks great.

JENNY
Thanks. The thing is, I wish I knew who I was fixing it up for, us or the next people to live here.

GREGORY
We're down.

JENNY
Oh, no!

GREGORY
No, I mean we're downstairs. I'll just carry her to her bed.

DEBBIE
I'm on my way.

GREGORY
Take your time. I've got her.

LALA
Maybe I could have a cigarette before we restart the oxygen.

GREGORY
Of course you can.

Act THREE, Scene SEVEN

Nighttime. LALA is awake and so is JENNY, who is coming to check on her.

LALA
Oh, hello. I was wondering if anyone was here.

JENNY
I'm here. I was wondering if you were awake.

LALA
I'm awake. It seems like I'm always awake at this time. What time is it anyway?

JENNY
Almost midnight.

LALA
Ah, the witching hour.

JENNY
Yes. I guess so.

LALA
Have you seen my family?

JENNY
Yes. I guess I have.

LALA
Where are they?

JENNY
Well, Gregory is at work.

LALA
Now? I never understood who takes a tour this time of night.

JENNY
No, he's not giving tours. He's guarding. Like doing security.

LALA
Oh. I hope it is not dangerous.

JENNY
I don't think it is. Mostly it's just quiet and deserted.

LALA
Have you seen Jenny or Debbie?

JENNY
Debbie's at home since it is nighttime. Jenny's here.

LALA
Because I wanted to talk to her.

JENNY
You can tell me.

LALA
Well, it's about Gregory. Do you know him?

JENNY
Yes.

LALA
I feel bad for him. I have one house and two daughters.

JENNY
Yes, me and Lynn.

LALA
Lynn and who?

JENNY
Jenny.

LALA
Yes. Anyway, I have nothing for him.

JENNY
He doesn't expect anything.

LALA
But isn't that the point of gifts? I'd feel better if I did something for him.

JENNY
You could.

LALA
I could? Like what?

JENNY
Well, he has been applying to film schools.

LALA
Did I know that?

JENNY
I think so. But he hasn't been getting accepted. He's gotten a couple of rejections.

LALA
My Gregory? From where?

JENNY
Columbia and NYU.

LALA
Well, they don't know anything.

JENNY
Well, you know, I went to NYU.

LALA
You did?

JENNY
Yes.

LALA
I think my daughter Jenny did, too. Did you know her?

JENNY
Yes, I know Jenny.

LALA
No, I mean did you know her there?

JENNY
Yes. I knew her in college, too.

LALA
Oh. I didn't know that. You seem older than her.

JENNY
But back to Gregory.

LALA
Oh, yes, Gregory. My grandson. I wish I could do something for him.

JENNY
I know. That's what we were talking about.

LALA
Oh. Did we come up with anything?

JENNY
Yes. I think maybe I have something. He did this acting thing at this film school in the city.

And they are a non-traditional school. They have programs that aren't two years long, aren't so expensive. Maybe you could send him to a film school that's one or two months.

LALA
Could I do that?

JENNY
Yes. I think you could.

LALA
And he would like that?

JENNY
Yes, I think he would.

LALA
I would like that, too.

JENNY
Good.

LALA
Thank you, Jenny.

JENNY
You're welcome, Mom.

GREGORY is in a spotlight, upstairs.

GREGORY
And that's where I was, my second day of film school. Actually, getting up early that morning, getting ready for classes.

LALA
Is anybody here? Deb-eeeee. Jen-eeee. Gregor-eee.

GREGORY runs downstairs. He is just out of the shower, half dressed.

GREGORY
I'm here. I'm here.

LALA
Oh, you're here.

GREGORY
I'm here, I was getting ready for film school.

LALA
Oh, that's right. You're going back to school.

GREGORY
Well, a program anyway. Thank you!

LALA
I wish I could be there. Is anyone else here?

GREGORY
Debbie will be here at eight.

LALA
And Jenny?

GREGORY
She's sleeping.

LALA
Can you wake her?

GREGORY
I'll try. Are you okay?

LALA
It's just, I don't know, something in my stomach.

GREGORY
I wish I could help you. I don't want to miss the train.

LALA
Oh, no. I don't want that either.

GREGORY
Would you like some coffee?

LALA
No. Maybe some tea? If it's not too much trouble.

GREGORY
No, I'll brew it while I get ready.

LALA

Thank you.

Lights change. GREGORY is upstairs trying to wake JENNY.

LALA

Father always liked those students of his. Grandfather had his wives, his children, his estates. Irving, he was a good man. But he died. Too soon. Who knows why?

GREGORY

Mom? Mom! It's time to wake up. Mother!

JENNY groans. Rolls over. Snores. Lights change again. GREGORY is running downstairs, dressed, rushing.

LALA

Gregory, is that you?

GREGORY

Yes, honey. It's me.

LALA

Where's Jenny?

GREGORY

She's upstairs. I couldn't wake her.

LALA

Oh, no, is she alright?

GREGORY
Yes. She's just asleep. And hard to wake.

LALA
Are you sure?

GREGORY
She's been that way all my life. I'll be right back.

He rushes to fix her tea.

LALA
Oh, Gregory, I wanted to ask you something. Gregory?

He gives her tea. Rushes out to grab his backpack. Puts some stuff into it.

GREGORY
I'm here sweetheart, what is it?

LALA
My stomach hurts.

GREGORY
I'm sorry. Mom won't wake up and I have to catch the train. Debbie will be here in about a half hour.

LALA
That long!

GREGORY
Would you like me to stay?

LALA
Oh, no, darling.

GREGORY
I can have Mom drive me later. Or be an hour late.

LALA
For school? Oh, no, darling. I wouldn't want that.

GREGORY
Okay, then I might literally need to run now.

LALA
You do that. I'll be fine.

GREGORY
I hope so.

LALA
When did you say Debbie will be here?

GREGORY
About 30 minutes.

LALA
And Jenny?

GREGORY
Mom is upstairs asleep. I couldn't wake her, but if you want to yell for her, maybe you'll have better luck.

LALA
No. Let her sleep.

GREGORY
You sure? You okay?

LALA
I'll live.

GREGORY
Good. I'll see you tonight. I love you.

LALA
I love you, too, darling.

He starts to leave, runs back and kisses her on the cheek and rushes out.

LALA
Oh, Gregory?

GREGORY
I have to go honey. I love you. See you later.

LALA
Is anyone here? Debbie? Jenn-ee?

Spotlight on GREGORY.

GREGORY
It was my second day of film school. We were in Union Square doing film tests. I had my juggling set with me, three bean bags shaped like UFOs. They were green, blue and yellow and they'd glow in the dark. I was clowning around for the camera, juggling, joking. I remember being happy ... happier than I had been for a long time ... happier than I would be again for some time. And maybe I felt something else.

Lights up on kitchen. LALA is in her chair.

LALA
Do we have any vodka?

JENNY
Yes, mother. There's some right there. In your shot glass.

LALA takes a big sip. Takes another.

LALA
Are there any cigarettes?

JENNY
Yes, mother.

LALA
Can I have one? Cigaretta, cigaretta?

                    JENNY
Yes, if the oxygen is off.

                    DEBBIE
I turned it off.

                    LALA
Oh, goodie.

JENNY lights a cig for LALA, hands it to her. She offers one to DEBBIE.

                    DEBBIE
No, Jenny. I have my loosies in my purse.

She goes into the hallway to find it.

                    LALA
Her what?

                    JENNY
She has a menthol cigarette in her purse.

                    LALA
But what did she call it?

                    JENNY
A loosie. Did you find it?

JENNY sticks her head out.

                    LALA
That's a funny thing.

LALA clutches her heart and slumps over.

JENNY
I told you, she buys them ... Mother? Mother! Debbie!

JENNY and then DEBBIE rush to LALA.

DEBBIE
Lala, Lala, can you hear me?

JENNY
Mother? Mother!

DEBBIE
Get her on the floor, Jenny. Lala, can you breath? Lala, breath.

JENNY
Mother can you hear me? Mother!

DEBBIE tries mouth to mouth.

DEBBIE
Come on Lala, come back to us.

GREGORY
My second day of film school. Maybe I should be grateful I had something to distract me.

Lights change.

DEBBIE

I'm sorry, Jenny.

GREGORY

I felt guilty. Being happy. Feeling free. I always felt that. If I took too much enjoyment in living life, it might be, I don't know, disrespectful of the dying.

DEBBIE is on the phone in the hallway.

DEBBIE

Yes, about an hour ago. No, the ambulance took her. Yes. Yes. Okay. Well, no. Yes, I said no. What do I mean? I mean, I'm going to sit here with the family for the rest of the day. Yes. Yes, fine. I'll be available for assignment tomorrow.

LYNN and JENNY sort things.

JENNY

I know you're anxious to settle things with the house, but Gregory and I were thinking …

LYNN

No way.

GREGORY

We put the house on the market. It sold in about six months. Leaving the house was like losing her again. I still miss her. And when I'm in Union Square, I still feel her floating over, looking to see what I'm doing. I still have the painting she saw her initials in. I never really learned to paint, and yet, there I am painting for her, painting to be with her. Painting.

END

The Sun

The Sun was first produced by Louis S. Salamone and TOY/After School Productions & Paper Tiger Productions on Feb. 4, 2004, at the KGB Theater in New York City, with the following cast, in order of appearance:

Andy Zenger ... Greg Klein

Angela Croton ... Victoria Beavan

Hank Lammarr ... Harry Perdon

Bryant Williams ... Jordan Deas

Matt Burke ... Joel Ginn

Set and lighting design by Josh Iacovelli. Publicity by Shawyonia Pettigrew and Michelle Michea/Aglaea Public Relations.

Cast Breakdown

ANDY ZENGER: Male, early 40s, editor of "The Sun," a sharp, clever man who has lost his way, turning his disgust with his success into failures, and has just hit rock bottom.

ANGELA CROTON: Female, 40s, very pretty, cynical woman from a rural area. Not book smart, but wise, except perhaps in love.

HANK LAMMARR: Male, 50s, open ethnicity, publisher of "The Sun, very much a suit.

BRYANT WILLIAMS: Male, early 20s, African-American intern from a nice suburb of Baltimore. The son in "The Sun," a Harvard journalism student on a hunt for information about his father's political fall from grace.

MATT BURKE: Male, 40s, good old boy editor-reporter with a dark side underneath. Charming, funny and probably racist and sexist, too. A heck of a good reporter, but morally challenged.

Act ONE, Scene ONE

Hagerstown, Maryland, 1997.

An office. Messy. It is a newspaper editor's office and all around it are remnants of old proof sheets and the finished products, some yellowing from age. There are book shelves along the walls, with awards and bound volumes and stacks of old papers. A three-quarter wrap around desk, a study old oak wood, dominates the room. A large-screen computer sits on the wrap around part of the desk. The main desk is mostly neat but the area around the computer is a mess, with the proof sheets and press releases and some fast food trash scattered around.

ANDY ZENGER, a disheveled man who fits the office, walks in carrying a tray of coffee and a bag of fast-food breakfast. He sets them on the desk. The clock on the wall says 6 a.m. Andy leaves and returns with a briefcase which he also places on the desk. Quickly, he takes a disk out of the case and pops it into the computer. We hear computer noises. He also pulls out a stack of papers and places them next to the computer, clearing out the old papers in the process. He dries up on a towel from same desk drawer, and then moves to a corner of the office where he reveals a small closet filled with shirts, ties, coats and pants. Quickly he changes into a suit and then cleans the office. Finally he settles into a balancing act of computer, coffee and biscuit.

At 6:30 a.m., a second person enters the office. Her name is ANGELA CROTON. She's bit older than Andy but looks like a good looking woman in her 30s. However, her voice reflexes her 20 years of smoking. She immediately begins taking pages from Andy to a paginating board outside Andy's office in the main space where she does paste-up work on them. The outer area is close enough that the two can talk freely.

                    ANGELA
Jesus Christ, not you again.

ANDY
I work here remember?

ANGELA
I'm trying to forget. And anyway, since when do I have to deal with you this early?

ANDY
I don't have a choice right now, what's wrong with you?

ANGELA
Maybe I'm tired of your drama.

ANDY
Says the passive-aggressive pot.

ANGELA
What does that mean?

ANDY
C'mon, I know you're not stupid. You just dumb yourself down to be with him.

ANGELA
That's where you lose me Andy. Your anger that you carry around at a guy who used to be your friend.

ANDY
He's not my friend. I'm beginning to wonder if her ever was.

ANGELA
Well, he's my friend, so it isn't going to help matters if you ...

ANDY
He isn't a friend. He manipulates. He hides behind his nice-guy 'I'm just a country boy facade.'

ANGELA
Do you have something to say? Something new?

ANDY
Yes, what the hell was last night about?

ANGELA
Last night?

ANDY
Stop doing that!

ANGELA
We were having a drink. That's what people do when they when they like each other. If you didn't run off like a child who didn't get his way, you could of had one, too. Or were you just rushing home to your wife?

ANDY
I had something to tell you.

ANGELA
What?

ANDY
I brought you coffee.

ANGELA
I don't need that Hardee's crap. You drop out of the coffee fund again?

ANDY
No, but I should. I paid $17 dollars last month. $17! And when it's my turn to buy and I forget, the press guys block my parking space and won't let me park til I buy. Fucking addicts. I think it'd be cheaper if we just pop white crosses.

ANGELA
Is that what makes you ornery?

ANDY
I think you know why.

ANGELA
I might know but I don't haveta like.

ANDY
Sure, there's some logic for you.

ANGELA
Don't mock me. And stay away from the paste up.

ANDY
I know. Union rules.

ANGELA
Were you using my knife?

ANDY
No, I brought my own.

ANGELA
I'da thought you'd be too busy writing the editorial to be messing up my pages.

ANDY
I just wanted to get a jump on things. Get some pages out of the way after Friday's fiasco. Editorial?

ANGELA
Shit, honey, I thought you knew. Johnny Case quit this weekend. Got an offer to work for Lighthouse.

ANDY
Just like that?.

ANGELA
He slipped his letter into Hank's office bout an hour after deadline.

ANDY
No notice and he splits in the middle of the night. What is he, the damn Colts?

ANGELA
The Colts left 15 years ago. Git over it.

ANDY
You can't trust anyone in this business.

ANGELA
Maybe they don't want to trust their lives to the unknown.

ANDY
Do you understand anything about newspapers?

ANGELA
I understand people. They're scared.

ANDY
They're cowards.

ANGELA
Don't call them that. They're my friends. Used to be yours too. Right now we know nuthin and that makes people scared.

ANDY
Hank said he didn't expect change.

ANGELA
Hank's just tryin to prevent panic.

ANDY
It isn't working. We can take bets who's next. It could replace the death pool. Anyway, I don't seem to be doing so well with Ronald Reagan.

ANGELA
You left a few papers in your time.

ANDY
So?

ANGELA
So, I've been here 10 years and I've seen 10 editors. You newspaper types are weird. I reckon if someone called from California or Kansas or some other place I've only seen on a map and offered you more money, you'd scatter too. Actually, I got a $20 says you're next.

ANDY
I'm not leaving here. You know that. I've married the area. Besides, I think there's newspaper execs all over the country that have nightmares about the dramatic lengths I went to, to burn my bridges in this business. Then they wake up in the morning and resolve never to offer me another job. Are you sleeping with him?

ANGELA
We're friends. Get over that, too.

ANDY
You must be sleeping with someone these days.

ANGELA
Nope, not even my husband.

ANDY
That's why I asked.

ANGELA
It is too early in the morning for the past Andy, don't start this. And don't you take yer frustrations out on me!

ANDY
You're the one who works with knives. But it seems like all you have for me these days is don'ts.

ANGELA
I got one more. Don't kill yourself for this. It ain't worth it.

ANDY
Even the rats have fled. Someone has to stay.

ANGELA
Matt'll be here. Of course.

ANDY
When they're printing nothing downstairs but Penny Savers and Military Tribunes, he'll still be roaming these halls.

ANGELA
Here's an idea: Why don't you take your anger out on someone else for a while, like Hank.

ANDY

Why?

HANK LAMMARR enters. He is the Sun's publisher, well dressed.

HANK

Andy, a minute?

ANGELA

I'll go check on the printer.

ANGELA leaves.

ANDY

I don't have much time. When were you going to tell me about Johnny?

HANK

I just got the letter myself. It shouldn't be too much of a problem.

ANDY

Not much, I'm already the editor and managing editor why not the editorial page editor too?

HANK

Nothing you can't handle. You've got the experience.

ANDY

Not doing it all at once.

HANK
We all have to work harder. I'm sure you'll do fine.

ANDY
It might help if you'd start replacing some of the people we've lost. We've got no M.E., no editorial, no correspondents, no photo editor ... oh, do you know what happened to the darkroom?

HANK
I meant to tell you, I sold our equipment to Zittlestown.

ANDY
You sold the darkroom to Zittlestown?

HANK
That equipment was more than 30 years old. We can't deduct it. Besides, we're going to save 70 percent on our new photo processing system.

ANDY
Great. When?

HANK
In a couple of years the digital equipment will be cheap enough to transform our system.

ANDY
So until then I guess I'll just design us to look like the Wall Street Journal.

HANK
Look, we've been over this. Just because their design style is 100 years behind the times, doesn't mean their opinions aren't valid. I've bought the staff point and shoots. I've got a deal on bulk color film and I worked out a printing deal with the Food Lion.

ANDY
The grocery store?

HANK
They have an amazing processor at the store on Wilson and Frederick. Better than we can afford.

ANDY
Then how do we afford it?

HANK
In return for our processing, they get 20 percent off all ads and inserts.

ANDY
And we get them back as a customer.

HANK
Take that, direct mail. They'll give us top priority and rush on deadline. Plus, we don't have to pay for those nasty chemicals and the equipment, so we more than balance out that 20 percent.

ANDY
And what if there's another scandal with their corporate? Jesus, Hank!

HANK
Plus, a few more clients like that and another resignation or two and we'll solve our budget problem.

ANDY
We're already understaffed. And why are we having budget problems anyway?

HANK
We had an extraordinary year of revenue last year. I overestimated what we'd take in this year.

ANDY
Hank, last year was an election year.

HANK
So?

ANDY
Ad revenues always go up in election years.

HANK
So?

ANDY
So, budget accordingly.

HANK
Right now I can't justify a drop in revenue. I had to project a 6% increase.

ANDY
An increase? You just said ...

HANK
I know what I said, but I had to make the numbers look good on paper. I still will by the time someone outside looks at them.

ANDY
At the expense of the staff?

HANK
Yes.

ANDY
The editorial staff?

HANK
I can't cut back on the ad staff. We need to sell ads. I can't cut back on the circulation staff. We need to distribute. I can't cut the press staff. They make half our money.

ANDY
We need reporters and editors, too.

HANK
They're not as important as you think.

ANDY
They're more important than you think.

HANK
We're paying thousands for that wire. Now I can justify it.

ANDY
We're homogenized shit. We're struggling to cover local and we have nothing original on state and national anymore. Too much AP just makes us look like every other paper.

HANK
People don't know the difference.

ANDY
I know the difference. The stories we pull are from the other papers in the state. AP just chops off the bylines.

HANK
You guys make plenty of money these days. We don't need to pay with bylines anymore.

Calculates and frowns.

ANDY
It's dishonest.

HANK
The news business is never dishonest.

ANDY
Except when it is.

HANK
Sometimes I don't think you understand this business.

ANDY
Like hell! I understand journalism.

HANK
But you don't understand the news business. You don't understand we run on a budget.

ANDY
I know budgets.

HANK
News budgets, maybe. I mean money. If we profit, you profit, too. You said yourself you have alimony payments to make. You have an ex wife, right?

ANDY
Two.

HANK
Ouch. I hope you have a Philadelphia lawyer, Mr. Zenger.

ANDY
No, but apparently both Mrs. Zengers did.

HANK

All the more reason for you to go along with this plan. If we have the year we're having, we're all gone. If we let a few more people leave and we hold off on replacing them, then we make budget, save our jobs and get a big bonus check.

ANDY

Hold off til when?

HANK

October. Just until the new fiscal year starts.

ANDY

I'm not staffing a newspaper until October on fumes and ghosts.

HANK

You should see your own problems clearer. You've got a new wife and two exes to support. How are you going to do that if you're unemployed? What if a chain decides local news is unprofitable?

ANDY

Holy shit. You're scared.

HANK

It's good business to be scared at this point.

ANDY
It's also good business not to piss the editor off. I need staff Hank. I'm killing my marriage trying to do this alone.

HANK
I won't let that happen. I've got just the thing for you. There's a young man in my office that's ...

ANDY
Oh, no. No more damn interns.

HANK
Don't take that attitude, Andy. He's here to help you.

ANDY
He's here for credit like all the others. It's bullshit, Hank. I'm asking you for professionals and you're giving me school kids.

HANK
He's got great potential.

HANK hands ANDY BRYANT's resume.

ANDY
I don't want him.

HANK
You don't have a choice. Besides he's a great kid. Honor student at Harvard.

ANDY
Now I really don't want him.

HANK
Andy, be reasonable. We couldn't all go to Maryland.

ANDY
Hank, why would a kid from Harvard work here?

HANK
He's from Baltimore. I guess he wanted to stay local.

ANDY
The Post would be more local than us.

HANK
He interned at the Post, last summer.

ANDY
Then why wouldn't he go back?

HANK
Maybe he gave Kate Graham sexual advice.

ANDY
I'm not taking him. Send him back to Harvard.

HANK
You have no choice.

ANDY
Interns sometimes don't work out. They run out of here screaming.

HANK
Don't Andy. Not this time.

ANDY
If he doesn't work out, you'll have to hire someone.

HANK
Just talk to him. You'll see. *(Uses ANDY's phone.)* Will you send Bryant into Andy's office? Andy, don't do anything stupid. You need this to work out more than me.

BRYANT WILLIAMS enters. He is a young, well dressed, preppy African American. He is obviously stunned by the mess.

HANK
Bryant, this is Andy Zenger.

BRYANT
Mr. Zenger. I'm pleased ...

ANDY
Andy.

BRYANT
What?

ANDY
Just call me Andy.

HANK
Andy!

ANDY
See?

BRYANT
Nice to meet you Andy.

HANK
I'll leave you two to get acquainted. Andy, I'll need the editorial ready when I get back from lunch, before I go to dinner. Bryant, good luck.

HANK leaves.

BRYANT
Good luck?

ANDY
Okay, journalist. What was wrong with that man's sentence?

BRYANT
The structure?

ANDY
No, the content.

BRYANT
He's going to be gone a long time, I guess, on deadline.

ANDY
Longer than you think. He's taking the life editor with him.

BRYANT
Did I need to know that?

ANDY
Yes. It means you have to watch what you say around her. Don't cuss him or anything.

BRYANT
Why would I cuss Mr. Lammarr? He hired me.

ANDY
Alright, let's take on a different story. A kid with a resume full of all the right things and affirmative action to boot decides to take a job at a 50,000 circulation in a small town in the hills. Why?

BRYANT
Affirmative action? I've gotten my stuff legitimately.

ANDY
I didn't say you didn't. I just said it was an option. Now answer the question.

BRYANT

What?

ANDY

Why?

BRYANT

Why what?

ANDY

Why are you here?

BRYANT

I thought I was here to intern.

ANDY

Leaving already?

BRYANT

I did research at the Post.

ANDY

And the Times?

BRYANT

I was an editorial assistant. That meant I fetched things.

ANDY

I'm concerned about your progress. You want to be a journalist, follow the trend. Sophomore year, Washington Post. Junior year, New York Times. Senior year, Hagerstown Sun. Did you cuss out Kate

Graham, Bryant, because we've all wanted to now and again, but trust me if you haven't already, don't, it doesn't work out so well. Other than that I'm here because I have alimony payments. Now why are you here?

BRYANT
I want to be a journalist, sir.

ANDY
Don't call me sir. Even if am I twice your age, I have half your pedigree. If a big corporation really does take over, I'm sure you'd be an asset to their statistics.

BRYANT
That's a load of crap.

ANDY
You get lots of crap here, Bryant. Look at us with the scavengers eyeing our presses. They don't tell you in class about publishers, or union rules, or corporate buzzwords. Last year, it was synergy. They were only late on that by half a decade. Fuck knows what they've got this year. Perhaps perspicacity.

BRYANT
That's it?

ANDY
You want more? Listen, it's never too late to change your major. There are more

respected lines of work. Lawyer. Crack Dealer. Whore.

BRYANT
Christ.

ANDY
I wish. You'll feel like a whore some days in this job but generally you don't feel so good. A criminal, sure. A scumbag, that's what the public says. A liar. A newspaper salesman. I hate that one. A fraud. But a writing whore? That's a achievement.

BRYANT
Are you done?

ANDY
For now. I'd go on, but deadline is half a day away and I have the work of three men to do. What about you? Are you staying or going?

BRYANT
I didn't drive an hour and a half to go screaming out of here. You can't scare me, Mr. Zen, uh Andy. That is what you are trying to do right? I am going to guess so because the alternative is to think of you as a hack, an asshole and a bigot.

ANDY
Think of me what you want. Everyone else in town has their opinion.

BRYANT
I'll reserve my opinion. I came here to learn about newspapers. I want to learn about deadlines. I spent two summers doing nothing but fetching lunches, editing and looking up bizarre facts. Do you want to know the GNP of southeast Asian countries? I can tell you that. But I can't tell you what it is like to have a byline in a real newspaper because I haven't gotten to write one story in my two internships. Why is my clip file sparse? Why am I here? The answer's the same. I want experience. I got the Times internship because I had already interned at the Post. But I turned down a second internship there, Andy, because I don't want bullshit jobs. I don't want to fetch things. Or research other people's facts. I want to be a journalist. A newspaperman. And I have skills. I can be an asset to a small understaffed paper. I can do the work of three men and more.

ANDY
That's great.

BRYANT
I think so. Do you still want me to run, Andy? I'm here and I will be all summer.

ANDY picks up the phone.

ANDY

Matt, can you come into my office when you get a minute?

MATT BURKE enters. He's a little older than ANDY but shorter, scruffier than Andy and in worse shape.

ANDY

Matt, this is Bryant ... uh, Bryant, our summer intern. Bryant, this is Matt Burke, our top news reporter and our temporary news editor. Matt, maybe Bryant here can ease your load a bit.

MATT

Ah hell, and here I was countin on the overtime. Gotta get another gun.

BRYANT

A gun?

MATT

They're talkin about outlawin Glocks now. Gotta get one 'fore they take 'em off the market.

BRYANT

What would you do with it?

MATT

Hunt deer. I'm kiddin. I dunno. Have it when the government tells me I can't.

BRYANT
But you're a ...

MATT
A what?

BRYANT
A reporter.

MATT
So?

BRYANT
I don't know, I guess I just expected you to be a ...

MATT
a liberal? *(BRYANT nods.)* Hell, boy, them's fightin words.

BRYANT
Boy?

MATT
Liberal?

ANDY
Jesus, you two deserve each other.

MATT
I've been in this business a long time now and I've seen all types of reporters. We might be a little left of center, to borrow a term from an old newsman, but you'd have to be stupid

or self servin to think we're really all Democrats and liberals.

ANDY
And I've never met a publisher who's anything but a fiscal conservative.

BRYANT
I guess I'm learning already.

ANDY
Well there you have it. *(To MATT.)* Just find something for him. We're in deep today, I'm short on copy and now I have to write an editorial on ... Shit, I've got to run after Hank. I'll be right back. Why don't you two get started?

ANDY leaves. MATT and BRYANT go into the newsroom.

BRYANT
It's good to meet you. Andy said nice things about ...

MATT
I reckon he stopped drinking agin then. I guess we can take you around town this afternoon, find you a beat to cover.

BRYANT
A beat!

MATT
I mostly do city council these days, although, truth be told, I'd rather someone else do it. I've got the county folks broke in better. But we're short staffed and there's glock money to be made.

BRYANT
Do you belong to the NRA?

MATT
Yup.

BRYANT
Weird.

MATT
Nah. There's all types of reporters really.

BRYANT
I guess. So is this Zenger guy really as much a jerk as he seems to be?

MATT
He mostly growls these days.

BRYANT
He sure did growl at me.

MATT
We get some pretty bad interns here. They want credit but not work.

BRYANT
Still, he said some things that were offensive. Racist even.

MATT
He's no racist, but he may have tried to scare you. Whatever he said, you'll hear worse out there.

BRYANT
Is Hagerstown that kind of place?

MATT
No more or less than any other. But people don't know how to deal with the press so they look shallow. It's stupid, but true. So I didn't get your full name.

BRYANT
Williams.

MATT
Bryant Williams? Where ya from?

BRYANT
Uh, here in Maryland.

MATT
Big state.

BRYANT
Maryland, not really.

MATT

Where in Maryland.

BRYANT

Oh, Baltimore.

MATT

Jesus ... Bryant Williams from Baltimore? What are you doing here?

ANDY enters.

ANDY

Just make something up today? Does he even understand what a stupid fucking ass he is? See, I don't call him that around the life editor. ... Matt, where's the water story?

MATT

In the news folder. Under, 'clusterfuck.'

ANDY

Anything happen?

MATT

Yeah, they said we have a water problem. As if we didn't know that.

ANDY

Anything else?

MATT

Nope.

ANDY
I've got a hole on the front and a page of nothing inside.

MATT
There's the wire.

ANDY
I hate that thing.

MATT
By the way, have you heard anythin?

ANDY
No. You?

MATT
Even my sources have limits.

ANDY
I know that.

MATT
Lighthouse or Airnet or Awesass.

ANDY
Narrows it right down.

BRYANT
Awesass would be cool.

MATT
Why do you say that?

BRYANT
They own sports teams.

ANDY
Wouldn't it be great to cover our own teams?

MATT
I'm waitin for the day one of the giants owns a nuclear plant or a tobacco company. Oh ... too late.

BRYANT
I'm not waiting for the day I am as jaded as you guys.

ANDY
I may be jaded, but at least I know how to interpret the news.

MATT
That's more than most people want to do. You know that.

ANDY
All I know these days is deadline.

MATT
Then you ain't no better than anyone else.

ANDY
Who said I was? I just said I need more copy. So get out there. Now!

ANDY retreats. MATT and BRYANT leave.

MATT
Okay, he can be a jerk, but I wouldn't take his job for all the glocks in the world.

BRYANT
He could be friendlier.

MATT
He could. Then again we could get out there. Don't worry about Zenger. Lord only knows where his head is these days.

The lights go down. When they come up, ANDY is at the computer. ANGELA enters.

ANGELA
How goes it?

ANDY
Okay. Better if they get me some copy.

ANGELA
Happy to have an intern?

ANDY
No. But he seems better than most.

ANGELA
He's nice.

ANDY
You used to think I was nice.

ANGELA
No I didn't. Broodin, funny, smart, maybe, but not nice.

ANDY
So then what did you see in me?

ANGELA
I saw a man who respected me. Who didn't take me for granted.

ANDY
That's nice.

ANDY goes to kiss ANGELA who hesitates then pulls away.

ANGELA
You can't have it like this, Andy.

ANDY
Why not?

ANGELA
You made a decision to get married. Now you have to live by it.

ANDY
I made a mistake.

ANGELA
If you made a mistake then you have to undo it. But you can't bring me into it.

ANDY

Why not?

ANGELA

Because she and I are friends.

ANDY

You aren't friends. She's an acquaintance of your sister in law.

ANGELA

So a reporter should know that she and I have lots of mutual friends.

ANDY

Do you know her well?

ANGELA

I know her well enough to know she's your type.

ANDY

My type?

ANGELA

Chirpy, pretty and tougher than you expected.

ANDY

Relationships are tougher than I expect.

ANGELA

I'm sorry you've been fighting.

ANDY
You and I never used to fight.

ANGELA
We never had the chance. We'd have sex or beer or both and then I'd go back to Pennsylvania for the other 90 percent of my relationship.

ANDY
The bad part. The unhappy part.

ANGELA
Don't say that. I love my kids and I'm tickled that I'm going to be a young grandmother and I love my job. I'm not miserable.

ANDY
Only in love.

ANGELA
I thought you would be happy with her.

ANDY
I was happy with you.

ANGELA
Don't you understand? I wasn't happy.

ANDY
I guess I don't understand.

ANGELA
I thought your marriage was going great.

ANDY
I like her. I just need a tutorial in living with her.

ANGELA
You spend all your time here.

ANDY
Do you know what happens when I go home? We fight about why I'm not home.

ANGELA
That's easy. Go home more.

ANDY
And then who gets this out every night?

ANGELA
Matt, for one.

ANDY
Yeah, Matt's always there to pick up the pieces.

ANGELA
Did I not just say don't start?

ANDY
I'm just saying I don't see what you see in him.

ANGELA
He's my friend.

ANDY
I saw you last night. You weren't acting like friends.

ANGELA
I'm not talking about this with you.

ANDY
You know he's shorter than you, right?

ANGELA
What does that have to do with anything?

ANDY
I'm just saying, in the grand scheme of bad choices, yours is somewhere up there with Woodward and Bernstein leaving the Post.

ANGELA
Who are Woodward and Bernstein?

ANDY
Good God. It's a stupid choice, that's the point. You know it is hard to have a conversation when ...

ANGELA
When what? When I'm not saying what you want to hear?

ANDY
When one person isn't expressing herself truthfully. Forget it, let's just try to make

deadline today. I can't afford another fine. How the fuck am I going to do this?

ANGELA
You jumped all over my last answer, so I don't know. Maybe your intern will surprise you.

ANDY
Yeah, and maybe Kate Graham will call and offer me another job.

BRYANT enters.

BRYANT
Matt'll be back in after city council. He said something new will break with the water board. I've got a couple of small stories for you from my new beat.

ANDY
What beat?

BRYANT
Chamber of Commerce.

ANDY
Ouch. And I the one who gets accused of hazing the interns.

ANGELA
Just ain't right. I'll laugh about that on my smoke break.

ANGELA takes her purse and leaves.

ANDY
So, Chamber of Commerce? Pretty exciting, huh?

BRYANT
It seems boring.

ANDY
No seems about it.

BRYANT
I guess you never know where you'll find the big scoop.

ANDY
I have a good idea where you'll never find it, but you'll pad your file and get free breakfast.

BRYANT
You ever break a big one?

ANDY
Nope.

BRYANT
That can't be true.

ANDY
What is truth?

BRYANT
Pardon my language, but bullshit.

ANDY
I like you much better with that language, but what exactly are you calling bullshit?

BRYANT
This pseudo-philosophy.

ANDY
Do me a favor: Use that word with Matt.

BRYANT
Will he understand it?

ANDY
Better than you can imagine.

BRYANT
He said you guys worked together before.

ANDY
Years ago, in Annapolis.

BRYANT
And you never broke a scoop together?

ANDY
A scoop sure. You said the big one.

BRYANT
I guess it depend on your definition of big one.

ANDY
That sounds like pseudo-philosophy to me.

BRYANT
I would say a scandal that indicts more than 30 politicians in five states is a big one.

ANDY
You know about that?

BRYANT
How in the world did you find out all those politicians were crooked?

ANDY
You know, sources, investigating.

BRYANT
Journalists don't make good sources do they?

ANDY
Nope.

BRYANT
But how did you get it, rather than someone else, the Post or someone?

ANDY
By being me, I guess.

BRYANT
So, you twisted words around until they said what you wanted?

ANDY
No.

BRYANT
You found someone willing to sacrifice his career to do what's right?

ANDY
What? No. Now what are you looking for anyway?

BRYANT
What?

ANDY
Yes, what. How do you know about Minergate?

BRYANT
It's famous. You must know that. It's in all the textbooks.

ANDY
I can't believe it's in the Chemistry books.

BRYANT
Listen, I want to be a reporter right? I want it enough to put up with your games.

ANDY
And?

BRYANT
And I thought it might help me to be around some famous reporters.

ANDY
So, this isn't random?

BRYANT
No.

ANDY
I shoulda known.

BRYANT
That's it?

ANDY
You're welcome to be around as long as you keep working.

BRYANT
But you don't want to talk about Minergate?

ANDY
Bryant, I think you'll learn a lot here. But I'm not a reporter anymore. You want to learn from a reporter, you go talk to Matt.

BRYANT
But he's so different.

ANDY
Aren't we all?

BRYANT
I guess so.

ANDY
I'll level with you. I was the junior reporter on the state line beat. I got a lot of background,. Matt had the experience. He found the evidence.

BRYANT
How?

ANDY
Wouldn't you like to know?

BRYANT
Yes.

ANDY
I guess you'll have to ask him.

Act ONE, Scene TWO

Afternoon.

MATT and ANGELA are in the newsroom.

ANGELA
Matt, I don't know about this.

MATT
What's to know? It's tradition.

ANGELA
It's also tradition that no one stays.

MATT
That's Andy's fault. You know how he is. Look how he acted last night.

ANGELA
Maybe he had a point.

MATT
What point? Acting like an ass to both of us? I'm tired of him acting like he's better than me. I broke that boy in.

ANGELA
You recommended him. You guys used to act chummy.

MATT
That's just what I'm sayin. I thought he'd make a good editor and he needed a job or he'd be flippin burgers. Does he ever thank me? No, ever since you came along, he's been an ass.

ANGELA
I didn't come along, Matt. I've worked here longer than both of you.

MATT
You know what I mean. Since you broke up with him.

ANGELA
He suspects.

MATT
He's still a reporter at heart. Deep down we can always sense when there's a good story lurking below the surface.

ANGELA
Then why are we lying to him?

MATT
He deserves it.

ANGELA
Why?

MATT
I told you, he's been acting like an ass.

ANGELA
But he's been doing that since we started lying to him.

MATT
So?

ANGELA
I don't get it is all.

MATT
No one asked you to get it.

ANGELA
What?

MATT
I'm sorry. I'm just tired of his games. I know him. I've seen him and his act for a lot longer than you. Trust me, he deserves this. He brought this on himself.

ANGELA
I'd rather just tell the truth.

MATT
Sure, in a perfect world.

ANGELA
I don't believe in that.

MATT
Listen, you were just a dumb fuck for him.

ANGELA
Why would you say that?

MATT
I didn't say that. That's what he told me.

ANGELA
How dare he.

MATT
I know! Why else would I say anything?

ANGELA
You didn't.

MATT
I know! Who would repeat such a thing?

ANGELA
That makes me so angry.

MATT
I don't blame you. I'm angry at him too. I mean, now you see why I've been angry.

ANGELA
I can't believe it.

MATT
Just think of how he's been acting.

ANGELA
Yes, but ...

MATT
Wait, here he comes. You know what to do?

ANGELA
Matt!

MATT
C'mon. Just do this for me.

ANGELA
Well ...

MATT
It'll just give him a scare. Maybe he'll run out of here and everything'll be ...

BRYANT enters.

BRYANT
Hey, what's going on?

MATT
... good.

ANGELA
Yeah, good. Okay, I'm gunna take my smoke break.

ANGELA leaves.

BRYANT
Was it something I said?

MATT
No, you know how addicts are?

BRYANT
How would I know?

MATT
I'm just saying, she needed her fix.

BRYANT
Okay, well I wanted to ask you something.

MATT
I've got to go. We're doing a drug bust later.

BRYANT
We?

MATT
The sheriff lets me ride shotgun when he busts dope dealers.

BRYANT
Oh, okay. Well, later.

MATT
Sure, what's it about?

BRYANT
You know, internship advice. Dealing with Andy.

MATT
Andy's simple. You just put up a front with him, tell him what he wants to hear, and who cares what he thinks when it all plays out.

BRYANT
What?

MATT
As for the internship, you're in a good place.

BRYANT
I'm sort of worried about that.

MATT
You'll get a lot of opportunities here. Things you couldn't do at the Post or Times.

BRYANT
How'd you know about that?

MATT
Andy told me. He actually said good things about you.

BRYANT
He did? I reckon he stopped drinking again.

MATT
Very funny. But I mean it. You'll get to write news and features and sports. You'll get to edit and design. Hey you can even do paste up. You ever laid out a page?

BRYANT
Well, in class. But at the paper they only let the tech people do it.

MATT
See? Good thing you're at a small-town paper then. Why don't you try. I think Angela left a couple of pages out there. They're even waxed already.

BRYANT
Really?

MATT
Yeah, go ahead try. Listen I gotta run, but we'll talk more in a couple of days.

BRYANT
You mean it?

MATT
Of course. I've got a night meeting tonight and some flex time tomorrow, oh and I have to go down to Annapolis the day after that for a vote, but after that. Sides, it's a long summer. Anyway, go ahead.

BRYANT goes to the tech board and starts to work on a page. MATT goes to leave but instead hides behind a huge file cabinet.

BRYANT
You're sure? *(BRYANT looks to MATT, but he is gone.)* Okay.

BRYANT picks up the pages and pastes them on the templates.

ANGELA enters.

ANGELA
What the hell do you think you're doing?

BRYANT
What?

ANGELA
You can't touch those pages.

BRYANT
I didn't know.

ANGELA
Are you using my knife?

BRYANT
It was the only one here.

ANGELA
That's a union knife. You're not even allowed to touch it, if you aren't in the union.

BRYANT
No one told me.

ANGELA
I'm going to have to report you.

BRYANT
Report me?

ANGELA
Yes. You've violated a half dozen rules already. Lord only knows, what else is there. There'll have to be an investigation, maybe a suspension and, course, a fine.

BRYANT
A suspension and a fine? All I did was lay down a page.

ANGELA
That's my job and don't you forget it.

BRYANT
I won't.

ANGELA
Oh, Jesus, I can't keep doing this. Matt? Damn it, Matt get out here.

MATT does appear, cackling like a 40-year old child.

MATT
Shoulda kept up with it. And you shoulda seen your face.

BRYANT
This was your idea?

MATT
Gotta learn to have a sense of humor in this business.

BRYANT
When I hear something funny I'll let you know.

ANGELA
I'm sorry, are you angry?

BRYANT
Uh, yeah.

MATT
Jesus, don't apologize to him. What kind of reporter apologizes?

ANGELA
I wouldn't know.

ANGELA goes to leave. She bumps into ANDY.

ANDY

Hey, what's wrong?

ANGELA

Nothing. I'm just going to lunch.

ANDY

Can we talk?

ANGELA

Not now.

ANDY

Later? Tonight?

ANGELA

Um, I've got to see my aunt.

ANDY

Tomorrow? This week?

ANGELA

I don't know. I'm busy this week.

ANDY

We're all busy. Between the deadline fiascoes and the defections ...

ANGELA

I'm late for lunch. I'll talk to you later.

ANGELA exits.

ANDY
Hey guys, what's going on?

MATT
You know, people and their drama. Pretty dumb if you ask me.

BRYANT
Yeah, like you weren't responsible.

MATT
Me? What did I do?

BRYANT
You ...

MATT
Never mind, I don't need no intern telling me how to behave. I'm going out to bust crooks.

BRYANT
I thought that was just a lie.

MATT
Me, I never lie.

ANDY
Not even when it's in your best interests?

MATT
Don't you start with me, Zenger. I'm not in the mood for you today.

MATT exits.

ANDY/BRYANT
Asshole!

ANDY
Well, see, you've been here a day and you're already learning.

BRYANT
I thought you two were friends.

ANDY
No, we haven't been friends for a long time.

BRYANT
Why do you work together?

ANDY
Not much choice.

BRYANT
You always have a choice.

ANDY
No, you have choices. You're a 20-something Harvard student with a high GPA and ...

BRYANT
Don't even say affirmative action to boot.

ANDY
The point is, I'm, a 40-something reporter turned editor who isn't likely to get another job and can't even enjoy his biggest successes.

BRYANT
Why? What happened with Minergate?

ANDY
I can't tell you that.

BRYANT
Why?

ANDY
It's complicated.

BRYANT
What?

ANDY
No, it isn't a what question. You might try how once in a while. In my experiences, how is pretty well underrated.

BRYANT
How?

ANDY
Too much focus on the Ws, I'd say.

BRYANT
Andy, is everything a joke to you?

ANDY
No, Bryant, coddling environmental polluters is not a joke to me. Neither is lying to the press or the press lying to the people for the establishment. Or publishers killing stories

when it serves the interests of their friend.
None of that is funny.

BRYANT

Look, all I want to know is ...

ANDY

I know what you want to know.

BRYANT

How?

ANDY

See! That's good, but in this case you want to ask who.

BRYANT

Andy ...

ANDY

Have you asked Matt?

BRYANT

After today? No way.

ANDY

That's too bad. That's exactly why you should.

BRYANT

Why?

ANDY
Because he tried to rattle you. Doesn't that make you curious?

BRYANT
Yeah, but you did the same thing.

ANDY
I tried to rattle a new intern. He tried to rattle Bryant Williams.

BRYANT
What?

ANDY
Exactly. Show him you can't be rattled and he'll break.

BRYANT
Are you sure?

ANDY
No, I'm not. But this time, it's you that doesn't have any other choice.

Act ONE, Scene THREE

Afternoon. A week later.

MATT and BRYANT are sitting around MATT's desk, feet up. MATT's desk has a toy construction truck on it.

BRYANT

No way.

MATT

No, seriously.

BRYANT

No way.

MATT

If it makes you feel better ... way. I got nothin to do this afternoon. Seeing as to what a good sport you are, go ahead and try me.

BRYANT

Any word?

MATT

You give me any word eight letters or more and I'll give you a better one to use of six letters or less.

BRYANT

Wonderful.

MATT

Great.

BRYANT

Obligation.

MATT

Duty.

BRYANT
Hippopotamus.

MATT
Pig.

BRYANT
Transcendental.

MATT
Shit.

BRYANT
Oh come on!

MATT
What?

BRYANT
I didn't ask for your editorial opinion.

MATT
I didn't give you one. Shit's transcendental. It's also much easier grasped by the average reader. Try another one.

BRYANT
Pseudo-philosophy.

MATT
Dogshit.

BRYANT
Dogshit? Why not bullshit?

MATT
Pseudo-philosophy isn't significant enough to be bullshit.

BRYANT
You know, you can't print shit.

MATT
You do on a slow news day.

BRYANT
I thought you double checked your sources on a slow news day?

MATT
You do. And pray for something more than shit.

BRYANT
Well, I could use something more than shit.

MATT
You ain't happy with your beat?

BRYANT
No, Matt. I'm going crazy with the Chamber.

MATT
That makes you sane.

BRYANT
It's boring, but not as bad as these photo assignments.

MATT
I take it you don't want the 7 p.m. ribbon cuttin?

BRYANT
No! Hell no! Why isn't there more news?

MATT
You got to get used to these slow news days.

BRYANT
I want something exciting. I want something fun. I want conspiracy. I want Woodward and Bernstein.

MATT
Jesus. And which one are you?

BRYANT
The Jewish one?

MATT
Listen, not everythin in journalism is All the President's Men. In fact, almost nothin in journalism is. That damn movie has turned everythin into a scandal. Somewhere, in search of a so-called scoop, some stupid reporter is doing an investigative piece on why his shit stinks.

BRYANT
Oh come on.

MATT
It's screwed up many a story. And caused the idiots to call everything -gate.

BRYANT
You covered a scandal or two.

MATT
Yes, sometimes, but if you go lookin for it, you'll fuck up.

BRYANT
So how do you get it then?

MATT
All I'm sayin is be patient. Develop your sources. They'll be there for you if they trust you.

BRYANT
Is that how you broke that story?

MATT
What story?

BRYANT
The mining story.

MATT
How do you know about that?

BRYANT
I read about it in a textbook.

MATT
I'm sure Andy will be happy we made Harvard j-school.

BRYANT
What's the deal?

MATT
No deal.

BRYANT
It's a surprise you guys ended up here.

MATT
Why?

BRYANT
You guys coulda gone to the Post or something.

MATT
I spent two years at the Times. Do you know how disturbing New York City is to a country kid? First chance I got a cut myself a deal with Many Media to get this job.

BRYANT
You left the Times to go to the Hagerstown Sun?

MATT
I got a great deal to come home. Trust me, you can't beat that.

BRYANT
And Andy?

MATT
He had an interview at the Post. It didn't work out.

BRYANT
Did he really cuss out Kate Graham?

MATT
I wasn't there, but word has it he did.

BRYANT
Why? For offering him a job.

MATT
Some people don't handle success well.

BRYANT
It's weird you both ended up here.

MATT
You're here. That's pretty weird. Interned at the Post and Times both and now in the hills and sticks of Maryland.

BRYANT
Maybe I can have a drink of that.

MATT
When do you turn 21?

BRYANT
September.

MATT
Sorry.

BRYANT
Oh come on.

MATT
You got any other questions?

BRYANT
Yeah, actually I have a few.

MATT
Seems like it. Whatever it is yer fishin for, you should just ask.

BRYANT
You broke a big scandal. I'm trying to learn. How you did it.

MATT
We heard rumors. Then we went out and proved them true.

BRYANT
How?

MATT
We had a source who confirmed what we knew.

BRYANT
My dad.

MATT
So, the truth is out. How's yer momma and daddy, Bryant Williams?

BRYANT
They're good. My dad says hi, actually. He said Matt Burke is a good man.

MATT
Is that what he said?

BRYANT
His exact words were, "Matt Burke is a man who you can trust with the truth."

MATT
Yer daddy's a good man.

BRYANT
Was he your source?

MATT
I can't tell you that, Bryant.

BRYANT
That's a non-denial denial.

MATT
No, it's a reporter's code. I've got to protect my source.

BRYANT
So, he was your source and that's why he had to abandon his career and ...

MATT
I didn't say that. Yer daddy didn't have anythin to do with the minin story.

BRYANT
Are you sure? Because if you think about it, it would make sense that even his party would never again support ...

MATT
No it doesn't and no he wasn't, ya hear? Listen, I gotta go.

BRYANT
You said you have nothing to do this afternoon.

MATT
I just thought of sumthin.

BRYANT
What?

MATT
You have to check your sources on a slow news day.

MATT rushes out.

Act ONE, Scene FOUR

The next morning.

ANDY is cleaning up as MATT enters.

MATT
It's still weird to see you in here in the mornin. At least this side of the mornin.

ANDY
It's not less weird being here this time of day. I never used to write editorials and design inside pages.

MATT
You got a minute?

ANDY
I have about 720 minutes before deadline and something to do with each one of them.

MATT
I know, and I'll be happy to help later, but I just wanted to give you a warning.

ANDY
Are they going into special session for the water problem?

MATT
Probably. Eventually. But it's not that. There's some things I want to say to you.

ANDY
Good, let's talk about the other night.

MATT
That's not what I'm talking about.

ANDY
Why not?

MATT
Because it is none of your business.

ANDY
Sure, a woman I'm in love with is none of my business.

MATT
She don't love you.

ANDY
You say.

MATT
Why would she? You're a married man.

ANDY
So are you.

MATT
This isn't about me.

ANDY
Actually, it is Matt. You betrayed me.

MATT
How did I betray you?

ANDY
I know you're not an idiot, so stop acting like one.

MATT
How am I acting like an idiot?

ANDY
With a chuckle and a grin and an aw shucks, I'm not the one we're talkin about here.

MATT
I didn't betray you.

ANDY
Yes you did, many times over.

MATT
Let's stick to the issue at hand.

ANDY
Fine. I've been honest with you about my feelings for her. I told you how much I loved her. And what did you do?

MATT
What did I do?

ANDY
You used my feelings against me. You manipulated her. You lied about your feelings,

to me and then to her, and acted like you were just being a good, magnanimous guy when all along you were just trying to get into her pants.

MATT
Me, what about you?

ANDY
Stop being coy.

MATT
I don't know what you're talking about.

ANDY
I guess you are an idiot then.

MATT
Fuck you, Andy. I'm outta here.

ANDY
Okay, have fun with Bryant.

MATT
Damn it, I knew you were behind that.

ANDY
Behind what?

MATT
Now who's being coy?

ANDY
He's been asking questions on his own. I guess Harvard teaches Minergate.

MATT
Don't call it that. You know how I hate that.

ANDY
You've lost your influence to make demands on me.

MATT
Andy.

ANDY
Bryant Williams. Tracking us down. Looking for answers about his dad. Undercover. Ironic huh?

MATT
This is not ironic.

ANDY
I don't know. Joe Williams kid turning into a j-student, that's ironic to me.

MATT
We have to get rid of him.

ANDY
I'm sure he'll leave if we tell him.

MATT
We can't tell him anything.

ANDY
I haven't decided to tell him anything.

MATT
You haven't decided. There's no decision to be made here.

ANDY
Maybe there's a moral issue here.

MATT
When the hell did you get a moral conscious? Last time I checked you were dating a state senator's secretary so you could steal secrets from the senator.

ANDY
I was undercover not covers, and I was breaking a story that needed to be told.

MATT
What the hell do you think I was doing?

ANDY
I think they call it ... felony destruction of evidence.

MATT
Fuck you. We agreed to let the past lie.

ANDY
It's lying.

MATT
You know all those years you disappeared with not a word and I thought you might be sore about this, but I don't give a damn, Andy. You kept it to yourself when you were down and needed a job. You should just keep it to yourself now ... more than ever.

ANDY
Is that a threat, Matt?

MATT
If I go down for this then you go down, too.

ANDY
Fine, but I'd just like to take this opportunity to say I told you so.

MATT
Fuck you, Andy. I've done nothing but good for you and this is how you act.

ANDY
No, Matt, a long time ago, you helped me, but you've been stabbing me in the back for a while and now I owe you nothing.

MATT
How did I stab you in the back?

ANDY
Shall we start with her and go back?

MATT
Leave her out of it.

ANDY
Fine, how about making me an accessory to a crime and a cover-up

MATT
I would be careful with your accusations.

ANDY
Why? What will you do? Have the sheriff lock me up and plant evidence on me?

MATT
You're asking for it.

ANDY
I know where the dirt is, Matt. You guys make a move on me and I'll get the feds in here on you.

MATT
Damn it, you're out of control. There's a logical way out of this.

ANDY
Oh great, I'm interest in hearing your logic.

MATT
We lie to him.

ANDY
I'm done lying for you

MATT
You said it yourself. You're implicated in this.

ANDY
So?

MATT
So you tell him the truth and you're going to jail, too.

ANDY
Maybe I can cut a deal.

MATT
Maybe ... but even then, you lose your career, maybe Angela.

ANDY
I thought we were leaving her out of it.

MATT
We can. We will if you forget all about it.

ANDY
I'm not forgetting.

MATT
Look, to this day I believe what I did was right.

ANDY
Right? We screwed up.

MATT
No, we didn't. We busted crooks. We shook up this region. And we did the right thing.

ANDY
What if we did the right thing the wrong way?

MATT
No such thing.

ANDY
Maybe his being here is a way to even the score. You know, karma?

MATT
You're talkin bout karma to a Presbyterian.

ANDY
Karma's a law of physics. And I'm talking about clearing my bad feelings by being honest with a person deeply affected by our actions.

MATT
Then there's something else you should consider.

ANDY
What?

MATT
This kid you want to help.

ANDY
What about him?

MATT
I actually like him. He's a good guy.

ANDY
So what? I like him, too.

MATT
Then you look him in the eyes and tell him his daddy's a crook.

END OF ACT ONE

Act TWO, Scene ONE

Two days later. Mid afternoon.

MATT is at his desk. Feet up, with dip and drink.

BRYANT
If you're done with your afternoon nap, it seems like I've got you.

MATT
Well I haveta go ta the ...

BRYANT
Magnitude.

MATT
Cosmos.

BRYANT
Are you sure?

MATT
You don't get the cosmos of it. Sure.

BRYANT
I don't know.

MATT
Well it don't pass the Harvard English dictionary, but I think it's better out here in the sticks.

BRYANT
People will get cosmos but not magnitude?

MATT
Think of people. They know cosmonauts who go into space which never ends. They hear magnitude and think it has to do with a compass.

BRYANT
I don't know.

MATT
Try again.

BRYANT
Congressman.

MATT
Rep. Geez kid make 'em hard. This getting to you? Yer sweatin a storm.

BRYANT
The air conditioning barely works here and it's 10 degrees hotter than Baltimore.

MATT
Less humid.

BRYANT
Great.

MATT
See, you didn't use wonderful.

BRYANT
Matt, I don't think this works. You never gave me a word for transcendental, a pig and a hippo are not the same thing and I don't think I'll ever say, I don't get the cosmos of it.

MATT
The point is keep it simple. You thought of hippo.

BRYANT
And you came up with pig.

MATT
I was raised on a farm. I guess at Harvard they teach you what's a pig and what's a hippo.

BRYANT
Not exactly. Where'd you go to school anyway?

MATT
Frostburg State.

BRYANT
Where's that?

MATT
Frostburg.

BRYANT
I didn't know that was a state.

MATT
It's not recognized in New England.

BRYANT
Hey, I was raised on the streets of Bal'mer.

MATT
You were raised in Roland Park and you spent your life in Prep School.

BRYANT
Hopkins Prep is on the streets of Bal'mer.

MATT
With a bright shinny fence around it.

BRYANT
We only stayed over there sometimes, but Nap town was cool.

MATT
It had its moments.

BRYANT
Like Minergate?

MATT
Don't call it that.

BRYANT
Why?

MATT
Because the sun does not rise and fall like a gate.

BRYANT
I don't know what you just said but it was poetic.

MATT
And not a word over seven letters.

BRYANT
So I guess we all lived there ten years ago.

MATT
Yup.

BRYANT
Then the miner ... stuff breaks and we all left.

MATT
Yup.

BRYANT
You came home. Andy went to Harrisburg, I think.

MATT
For a while. Then he went to the desk.

BRYANT
I've always wondered why he quit.

BRYANT waits for an answer and doesn't get one.

BRYANT
Yeah ... You guys could have written your own ticket.

MATT
I reckon you could say we did, Bryant.

BRYANT
Dad came back to Roland Park. I've always wondered why he quit.

MATT
Yeah?

BRYANT
Yeah ...

BRYANT waits for an answer and doesn't get one.

BRYANT
He had a plan. From the state house to the House to the Senate. He had good party support. Ambitions. Good fundraising. Then one day he quit and never returned.

MATT
He's got a good law practice. Makes a lot of money. Maybe he just didn't like politics.

BRYANT
No, he loved it. You should know that. He even talked about being the first black president.

MATT
I think I heard him say that once or twice.

BRYANT
Then it wasn't that he didn't like politics. He left politics right around the time you left to come here.

MATT
You said that.

BRYANT
I thought you might know why my father left politics.

MATT
I dunno. Maybe he got sick of it or somethin.

BRYANT
We just went through that. He left for some other reason. I think maybe it had something to do with miner, um, the miner story. I have a theory that he was a source and his involvement doomed him in politics. I mean, think about it, more than half the people convicted were Democrats. His own party would have deserted him.

MATT
I told you I can't tell you my sources.

BRYANT
No?

MATT
No! A man's gotta duty to protect his source.

BRYANT
Okay, let's try it this way. If my father was your source, don't say anything. I'll count to ten and ...

MATT
Oh, no. Uh-un. Yur not gunna git me on Watergate. You can try all your college crap but yur not gunna git me on Watergate.

BRYANT
Matt, I still don't understand what your problem is with Watergate.

MATT
That movie ruined journalism.

BRYANT
You know, it was more than a movie.

MATT
It wasn't such a bad story, but it screwed up everythin as a scandal.

BRYANT
So, I guess I can't call you deep throat.

MATT
Why the hell would you?

BRYANT
I need information. You could be my source.

MATT
I can't be your source. Your father, uh ...

BRYANT
My father what?

MATT
um, he wouldn't approve.

BRYANT
Wouldn't approve of what?

MATT
Uh, he never liked Watergate either.

BRYANT
Damn it, I'm sick of these games.

MATT
This ain't a game, Bryant. It's professional ethics.

BRYANT
Do you know how many letters are in that word?

MATT
Twelve. Eighteen if you count the whole damn phrase.

BRYANT
It's what you call dogshit.

MATT
I know why you feel that way.

BRYANT
I remember you, Matt Burke. You used to come over to the house, back in Naptown. You'd huddle with my dad for a while and

you'd both be all ash faced. Then we'd all go out back and toss the football or grill food and act like everything was normal. Then you'd huddle some more. One day the story broke and the next my dad quit the state house. Funny how we never saw you again after that.

MATT
Bryant, I don't owe you any answers.

BRYANT
Yes, you do.

MATT
You wanna be a reporter, Bryant, then you have to learn a few things. If yer daddy was my source, then I havta protect him. And if it wasn't Joe, then I have to protect someone else. Either way, I have a duty and it ain't to you. *(MATT begins to pack his photo bag. He takes a gun from a locked drawer and puts it into his photo bag.)* I'm fixin to go out on patrol with the sheriff.

BRYANT
I still have questions.

MATT goes to leave.

MATT
I don't doubt it, you been so busy making speeches, you haven't gotten around to asking the simple stuff. Do they ever tell you

in Harvard to just cut the crap and ask a question?

BRYANT
Huh?

MATT
I guess that's graduate school. See you later.

Act TWO, Scene TWO

Near deadline. A week later.

ANDY is working at his computer, ANGELA at the tech board. BRYANT is sitting and MATT is standing mid-speech.

MATT
And if no one agrees, then we've got a depleted watershed and four dry states. But we have it as bad as any of them.

BRYANT
Oh my goodness.

ANDY
Um, is there any way you can write the editorial?

MATT
Sure. I've got everything else filed.

ANDY

Good. I've still got pages to paginate and you know the details better anyway. Do you want to talk to Hank?

MATT

I have, but I reckon I will agin.

HANK enters. He has a press release with him.

HANK

Good, everyone I need in one place. Keep working. This will just take a minute. We need to run with this.

MATT

What?

HANK

The buyout.

ANDY

Who?

HANK

Airnet.

MATT

Jesus Christ, they already own the papers in Frederick, Shepardstown and Gettysburg.

HANK
Exactly, and they have been our best press customer since the Frederick press broke down.

ANGELA
Wholly shit.

HANK
That's a good way to put it, but I'm sure we'll all come out fine. Airnet's regional holdings give us a great chance for corporate synergy and perspicacity.

ANDY
You want this tonight?

HANK
I know, it's breaking on deadline, but we can't get scooped on our own sale. Matt?

ANDY
Matt's working on the Water Board editorial.

BRYANT
I can do it.

HANK
Andy is that okay? *(ANDY nods.)* And to think, you didn't want an intern. Bryant, here's the press release and a number for an Airnet spokesman. I'll give you a quote in a minute.

BRYANT

Cool. You won't be sorry.

BRYANT takes the press release and exits to the newsroom.

MATT

Hank, what does this mean?

HANK

Too early to tell. But that's not important now. We'll figure it out off deadline. Andy, there's one more thing. Let's walk to my office (ANDY and HANK exit through the newsroom.) How's your resume?

ANDY

Fine.

HANK

I'd get it ready.

ANDY

It's always ready.

HANK and ANDY exit.

MATT

Well, now we know.

ANGELA

Matt, do you believe what Hank said about no changes here?

MATT

Do you?

ANGELA

No.

MATT

Me neither. When a new group comes in they make changes. We're safer than them, you're safer than most.

ANGELA

Why? And who are we safer than?

MATT

They aren't movin those presses, so they'll always need someone to tech the pages. They need bosses, too, course they usually prefer their own.

ANGELA

Oh my God. Andy'll be fired.

MATT

He will, but I don't like how that sounds.

ANGELA

Matt, I ...

MATT

You know you can't do this agin?

ANGELA
To tell the truth, I don't know. I don't know anythin right now, Matt.

MATT
You can't make a bad marriage good by cheatin, and even if you could, yer not gunna get anywhere close to happiness with Zenger.

ANGELA
Am I getting anywhere near happiness now?

MATT
What the hell does that mean?

ANGELA
I'm tired of cheating. I'm tired of lies.

MATT
You lost your right to morality when you started cheating on your husband.

ANGELA
It's easier to talk about morality when your judgin someone else's.

MATT
What the hell does that mean?

ANGELA
What about your morality?

MATT
We're not talking about me.

ANGELA
No, we never are. You're just the guy who knows best for everyone else.

MATT
I do.

ANGELA
Well, don't judge me Matt. This ain't as simple as right or wrong, black or white, true or false.

MATT
I'm not judgin you. I'm just givin you advice.

ANGELA
I don't want it.

MATT
It's good advice.

ANGELA
I'm sure it is, but it's your view. I'm startin t'think I need to figure out mine on my own. And I know one thing already. We're through.

MATT
Andy, was right about you. You are just a dumb fuck.

ANDY enters.

ANDY
E tu Brute? How's that editorial?

MATT
I think I've done all I can. I'll get the copy and run it to Hank.

MATT leaves. ANDY picks up his phone and pushes a button.

ANDY
Bryant, how's it going? Good. Get in here.

BRYANT walks in. He's sweating.

BRYANT
Hey, it's under "the Sun."

ANDY
I found it, thanks.

ANGELA
What kin I do?

ANDY
Just stand guard. Deadline story or not, we're gunna make it today.

ANGELA
How long til yur done?

ANDY
Less than five.

ANGELA
I'll be waitin for it.

ANDY
Thanks, Angel eyes.

ANGELA
You remember that?

ANDY
"What did I do, what did I say?" How could I forget?

ANGELA
It's been a long time.

ANDY
Let's get this to bed and then we'll get a drink.

ANGELA leaves.

ANDY
How'd everything go?

BRYANT
Great. It was as easy as the chamber stories.

ANDY
As scary, too. We're pasted in. Good work. Not a bad clip for you either. Breaking news.

BRYANT
Thanks. Can I have a drink, too?

ANDY
Sure, why not?

BRYANT
No, ID, remember?

ANDY
Not a problem. We'll finish up and then go for celebratory drinks.

BRYANT
I also need to talk to you.

ANDY
That's fine, but let's celebrate now, and be serious later.

BRYANT
What exactly are we celebrating?

ANDY
Perspicacity.

Act TWO, Scene THREE

Early morning, hours later.

ANDY's office. ANDY and ANGELA enter.

ANDY
I thought we'd never get out of there.

ANGELA
You used to love to socialize with the staff.

ANDY
We used to have a full staff. It was almost nice being their editor.

ANGELA
Almost?

ANDY
You know. The deadline rush. The breaking story. The big scoop.

ANGELA
You make it sound like the past.

ANDY
It is. I got fired today.

ANGELA
You got fired?

ANDY
The truth is Airnet's plans here don't call for an editor here. They said they'll try to look around for something else for me or give me a package, whichever.

ANGELA
Oh my God, Andy. I'm so sorry. I shudder to be askin this but how 'bout me?

ANDY
You're fine. They're gunna need to hire more tech people, not fire the ones they have.

ANGELA
What did you tell Michelle?

ANDY
I haven't told her anything, yet. She's staying at her mom's.

ANGELA
Oh my God. Andy what happened?

ANDY
Tough being married to the paper. I should learn my lessons.

ANGELA
Matt said you had issues.

ANDY
Matt said that?

ANGELA
I don't know why I'd believe him now anyway.

ANDY
What are you doing with him?

ANGELA
What?

ANDY
Why did you do that to me?

ANGELA
He said you were unethical. He said you were putting one over on me.

ANDY
What? What a hypocritical son of a bitch.

ANGELA
He'll kill you if you talk about his momma that way.

ANDY
Stop defending him. Why does he have to fuck up everything good in my life?

ANGELA
That's not what he was doing.

ANDY
It's what he's done. Over and over and continues to do to this day.

ANGELA
Andy, did you call me a dumb fuck?

ANDY
What? No.

ANGELA
God, maybe I am. I can't believe I'd believe his lies.

ANDY
Don't worry, we'll get him back.

ANGELA
There's nothin you can do.

ANDY
Yes, there is. Listen I promised I'd talk to him.

ANGELA
Who?

BRYANT enters.

BRYANT
So here's where you disappeared to.

ANDY
Oh, yeah, advice. Sorry, I forgot.

ANGELA
And now, it's my turn to disappear.

ANDY
Don't go. Just give us a minute. *(ANGELA leaves.)* Sorry, I was working on ...

BRYANT
Divorce number three?

ANDY
Yeah, I guess, so. And you were working on the story of your father leaving politics.

BRYANT
You know that?

ANDY
C'mon Bryant, I helped bust 35 crooked politicians and one environmentally-hazardous and morally corrupt mining company. You think I can't connect a father and a son?

BRYANT
Did Matt tell you?

ANDY
I told you to talk to him, remember?

BRYANT
You did, but he wouldn't talk.

ANDY
I know. I knew he wouldn't talk to you.

BRYANT
You knew? Why didn't you tell me.

ANDY
Did you come right out and tell us what you were doing?

BRYANT
Fair enough. Damn it. I tried everything with him too. The Goss. The Yak Yak.

ANDY
I don't think I want to know.

BRYANT
Interview techniques ... from Reporting 101.

ANDY
Bryant, this isn't Reporting 101.

BRYANT
Andy, this may be a joke to you, but it's my life ...

ANDY
It's my life, too, Bryant. Ten years of it.

BRYANT
I'm tired of your chicken-shit games. I need to know what you know.

ANDY
Tell me what you know.

BRYANT
What?

ANDY
Let me see where you are. If you're lost, I'll point you in the right direction.

BRYANT
You know what I know. My father had a promising political career and suddenly he left politics for good to go back to lawyering.

ANDY
What did he say about it?

BRYANT
Politics didn't suit him.

ANDY
You believe him?

BRYANT
He's never been one to lie to me, but I know that's not true. I was only 11 when he quit, but I can remember him being sad. Depressed even.

ANDY
A man who loved politics, I'd say.

BRYANT
Yeah. But he quit in '88 after you guys broke that story.

ANDY
Minergate.

BRYANT
I think I agree with Matt. Could we be more intelligent and original than to call every big story Gate?

ANDY
Fine, you name it.

BRYANT
Let's call it the Crooked Line.

ANDY
It doesn't fit as nicely into a headline ... but, fine, what the hell. Tell me about the Crooked Line.

BRYANT
A shady company called Allied Mining, set up a dummy corp called Mine Own to lobby for permits that Allied couldn't get. Mine Own promised to forgo strip mining and revitalize mine towns but instead they continued Allied's destruction of the Appalachias. A reporter named Andy Zenger stumbled upon this information while romancing a state rep's secretary.

ANDY
Hey! That is not true. It was a state senator's secretary and I don't think that was in the clippings.

BRYANT
It screamed it from the byline.

ANDY
You sound like my ex-wife's lawyer.

BRYANT
I certainly could use the money ... which, by the way, was what Allied-slash-Mine used to hide their shaky permit fixing.

ANDY
I can't believe I get to say this. Follow the money.

BRYANT
Enough with Watergate!

ANDY
Clearly it's valid here.

BRYANT
Fine. Allied-slash-Mine spread around hush money. They were slick. Most of it was legal. Morally questionable, but not to American politicians ... or the American public apparently. Except as it turns out, there was a lot of illegal deals too. Somehow you got a hold of a slush list and documented illegal payments to politicians in five states. Congressmen. A Senator. Even a Governor. All of whom went to jail along with several Allied officials.

ANDY
You almost make me proud. Although no one went to jail for long, and the Supreme Court has now ruled bribes are free speech.

BRYANT
How did you get the slush fund list?

ANDY
I didn't.

BRYANT

Andy, don't keep playing games with me.

ANDY

I didn't get the sheet. I found out several state senators and reps in Maryland were on the take. Matt dug from there until he learned there was a golden lawyer's pad filled with names and the number of dollars they'd been given. Matt also learned which Allied official had the list. Then he called in a favor and got the list.

BRYANT

I don't understand.

ANDY

Allied's offices were out here. The official never let the list out of his briefcase, but Matt had him arrested and took the list out of the briefcase himself.

BRYANT

Arrested, for what?

ANDY

Drunk driving.

BRYANT

What? I still don't understand. Was he drunk?

ANDY

No! He was being detained so Matt could get the evidence.

BRYANT
That's one hell of a favor. Was his friend the sheriff, because ...

ANDY
Bryant, I think you're missing the point.

BRYANT
What point?

ANDY
Who?

BRYANT
At the risk of sounding like you, who what?

ANDY
Bryant, what have you been trying to find out all this time? Who told us about the evidence? Who was our source?

BRYANT
My Dad!

ANDY
Your dad.

BRYANT
Oh my God, this is great! This is exactly what I wanted to hear! I can't believe it! I've got to call Mr. Amburg. I'll wake him, but he won't mind. Can I quote you on all of this?

ANDY
Quote me on what? Who's Amburg?

BRYANT
My publisher. Oh my God, I have to call him! I need to go call him!

ANDY
Your publisher? *(ANDY stands.)* I think it's time you tell me why you're here.

BRYANT
Listen, don't get upset. You know the story too. I wanted to do something for my dad. I hated that he seemed so unhappy while I was growing up. I started looking for microfilm from his term. It didn't take much looking to find your bylines.

ANDY
And I guess it didn't take much logic to connect it all to a publisher.

BRYANT
I'm sorry if you feel used, but ...

ANDY
Fuck used, Bryant. I don't feel used. I feel dirty.

BRYANT
It's not dirty. It's for a real story.

ANDY
By a son? Who decided his facts before he had the evidence?

BRYANT
Okay, it's not objective, but who cares? You told me it's true.

ANDY
No, that's not what I said.

BRYANT
I'm tired of your words. I have a story to write.

BRYANT starts to leave.

ANDY
You dad wasn't a hero Bryant.

BRYANT
Now you're lying.

ANDY
He took Allied's money. He was on the list. And what's more, he was one of the reps my secretary friend fingered. Matt pressured your dad til they worked out a deal.

BRYANT
Bullshit.

ANDY
Why do you think he resigned?

BRYANT
This isn't right. My dad isn't a crook. He was taken down in the wake of the scandal. His own party turned on him. More Democrats went down than Republicans. Of course they turned on him. They always do. I had this all figured out.

ANDY
You had it figured out except for the facts.

BRYANT
If my dad was on the list, then he would have been indicted.

ANDY
The guy that kept the list was incredibly anal. I guess he'd have to be to keep a list like that. Anyway, he alphabetized it. Later, in court, he said he shredded the un-alphabetized version, but only because it was disorderly, not because it was illegal. Course, he went to jail, too.

BRYANT
I'm completely lost.

ANDY
Matt took the last page. Ripped it clear out of the yellow pad, balled it up and tossed it in the bay. No one ever noticed. You find few office holders among the Xs, Ys and Zs.

BRYANT

And Joe Williams ...

ANDY

His name never came up. Neither did David Wilke's by the way. Or Lonnie Wendell's. Gov. Wendell still favors strip mining down in West Virginia. We'll see what happens if he gets the presidential nomination in 2000.

BRYANT

Why can't you take him down?

ANDY

There's no evidence. Matt destroyed it and it isn't like the mining guy was going to admit to more bribings.

BRYANT

How do I write this? If I tell the truth it ruins my father not to mention you guys and if I don't, then I'm in a cover-up and what's more I have to break a contract with a publisher and pay him back thousands of dollars.

ANDY

Pay him back what?

BRYANT

I took an advance.

ANDY

Shit.

BRYANT
Ten thousand. I spent a lot of it too.

ANDY
You could call it research money.

BRYANT
Do you see my car Andy? Do you see what I'm wearing? That's where my research money went.

ANDY
Business expenses.

BRYANT
You don't get it. To fulfill my obligation to my publisher, I have two choices: screw my father with the truth about his criminal activity or lie and screw my reputation and perhaps future by participating in a coverup.

ANDY
Don't do either.

BRYANT
What do I say to the publisher?

ANDY
Tell him you found proof your father wasn't the source

BRYANT
What proof? If I tell him who the source is, then I'm giving him a different story to write.

And if I don't know the source, how can I rule out my father? And anything I say is a lie anyway.

ANDY

Bryant, you wanted to know the truth about your dad and why he left politics. Now you know. What you do with this information is another story.

BRYANT

Does it worry you? You could go to jail. You could be ruined.

ANDY

I guess I took the risk because I thought you should know.

BRYANT

Why?

ANDY

Everybody lies, Bryant. Sometimes we call it criminal and sometimes we say it is in our best interests. I've told a lot of lies, to a lot of people close to me, and I'm still telling lies. The truth is, I'm just tired of it.

BRYANT

What do I do?

ANDY

I don't know.

BRYANT
Do you think you'll have an idea soon?

ANDY
Yeah. You'd better go home and talk to your dad.

BRYANT
Andy, I'm in shock. I don't know what's true anymore.

ANDY
Neither do I, Bryant. Neither do I.

BRYANT leaves.

ANGELA steps back in.

ANGELA
What the hell did you just do?

ANDY
Huh?

ANGELA
He just went tearin out of here like he seen the dead rise.

ANDY
No, he saw the risen die.

ANGELA
What?

ANDY
Do you believe Matt?

ANGELA
No, not anymore, but Andy ...

ANDY
I know.

ANGELA
No, I don't want to cheat anymore.

ANDY
I don't either.

ANGELA
I want to do this right. A divorce. An honorable man to be a step-father for my kids.

ANDY
I can be honorable.

ANGELA
I want you to settle things with Michelle.

ANDY
So would I.

ANGELA
So we should be waitin then.

ANDY
That's true.

ANDY and ANGELA slowly drift into a kiss.

Act TWO, Scene FOUR

The next day. Saturday. The office is deserted except for ANDY who is packing. A door down the hall slams. MATT enters.

MATT
What the hell do you think you're doing?

ANDY
Rhetorical?

MATT
I just got off the phone with Joe Williams. You told him everything?

ANDY
I told him everything. Did he tell you everything?

MATT
That Bryant was hired to write a book. Yeah, he told me.

ANDY
So, we're clear.

MATT
Yeah, we're clear as a corn field during a winter's full moon. How could you do this?

ANDY
How could I not, Matt?

MATT
You protect a source.

ANDY
Well, fuck, Matt, he wasn't my source.

MATT
He was. He was the source to the story.

ANDY
He was your source to my story. Minergate was my story.

MATT
Don't call it that.

ANDY
It's my fucking story I can call it whatever I want whenever I want to whomever I want. Maybe I should call Kate Graham and tell her she was right about Lonnie Wendell and Minergate.

ANDY goes to the phone. MATT pulls out his gun.

ANDY
Jesus, Matt, no. It's not worth it.

MATT
I never shoulda trusted you. Not this time when you came looking for a job and not ten years ago with the story.

ANDY
Put the gun down, Matt. There's still a way out of this.

MATT
Uh, un. You done exposed it.

ANDY
No. I didn't. He's not going to tell anyone.

MATT
I'm not goin to jail.

ANDY
No one said anything about jail. For that to happen Bryant's got to write a lot of dirt about his dad. What are the fucking odds of that happening?

MATT
Damn it, there's should be no odds. You just broke a sacred code, screwed up a boy's relations with his dad and maybe landed our asses in jail. Why the fuck would you do such a thing, Andy?

ANDY
Maybe I wanted to tell the truth for a change.

MATT
You should known by now, Andy. Truth is like an eye-witness account.

ANDY
All your slogans and nonsense sayings and farm logic, can't change the facts. I told that young man what he was entitled to hear.

MATT
The truth?

ANDY
Yeah, it may have been harsh and it may not have been wise, but for once, I did it, and it felt good.

MATT picks up the phone and dials.

MATT
Fine. Let's see how you like the truth.

ANDY
What are you doing?

MATT
I'm calling your wife and telling her about you and Angela.

ANDY
What?

MATT
I drove by your place last night, saw her car. If I hadn't had my wife with me I'da popped you both then. *(Into the phone)* Hi, ma'am. This is Matt Burke from the paper. Yes, I know, awful. That's why I called. Is she there? Please let me say hi, I have news for her.

ANDY
Matt, Jesus, no.

MATT
Does it feel good now, Andy? Let me practice this truth thing. 'Hey, Michelle, I don't know if you knew, but your husband and the woman that set you up with him had an affair, and since you're out of the house, it seems that they're gunna go right back to ...'

ANDY screams and charges MATT.

MATT SHOOTS. HE HITS ANDY IN THE ARM. ANDY FALLS.

MATT
Oh, wholly fuck. Our mother of God, what have I done?

ANDY
You shot me you son of a bitch.

MATT
You call my momma a bitch and I'll shoot you again.

ANDY
I apologize for what I said about your momma. But she sure did raise a bastard. I can't believe you killed me. Someone tell her I love her.

MATT
Your wife?

ANDY
No, Angela.

MATT
You can tell her yourself. I hit you in the arm.

ANDY
Well, if you kill me now.

MATT
I'm not gunna kill you.

ANDY
Well you sure did do a good job of pretending.

MATT
Andy, if he writes this book, we're in jail.

ANDY
He won't. And if he does, will he tells the truth? And even then, we can always deny it.

MATT
Yer on the record.

ANDY
I'm on deep background. If he uses my name, I'll just call him a liar.

MATT
Just like deep throat.

ANDY
Exactly. Besides, last I heard the evidence was in the Chesapeake.

MATT
That was a long time ago, huh? It'll be in the Caribbean by now. We better get you outta here.

MATT helps ANDY to his feet, and they begin to leave.

ANDY
Thanks. Listen, I really grew fond of Bryant. And I stressed to him what happens if he writes this. I don't think he will. But there is one thing?

MATT
What's that?

ANDY
How are we gunna cover up this?

MATT
Not hard. A lil carpet cleaner. Country doctor. As long as no one heard us.

ANDY
No, the presses downstairs are moving with the Frederick Sunday edition. Drowns out everything. And you know how deserted this place is on Saturdays.

MATT
So, there's just the hole in your arm. You might have to hide it from your women for a few days.

ANDY
I'll just tell people her husband came home. That's plausible.

MATT
Her husband came home. Sure. That's true enough. Wasn't that Carol in Essex?

ANDY
Shelia in Glen Burnie.

MATT
I coulda gotten you outta that one easy.

ANDY

Easier than throwing the documents in the Chesapeake?

MATT

This is the last time I ever tell you this ... I did what had to be done to get us a scoop.

ANDY

I know you did.

ANDY and MATT exit.

BRYANT steps out from behind the big file cabinet.

BRYANT

Oh my God. I can't believe Andy was right. *(BRYANT picks up the phone and dials.)* Mr. Amburg, it's me. No, no, it wasn't him, but I've got something even better. Yeah, of course. I'll give you the lead. What if Woodward and Bernstein washed out and hated each other? Oh, they do? Okay, well, I'll go you one better. What if they were covering up something themselves? Yes, okay, we'll see when they reveal who it was, right? Okay, one more try. What if Bernstein shot Woodward trying to keep that secret safe? Yeah, I thought you'd like that one. I'll be in tomorrow.

Act TWO, Scene FIVE

The next Monday. Late afternoon.

ANDY's office. ANDY'S ARM IS IN A SLING. ANDY IS PACKING. All of his furniture is already gone. He is picking from scattered remains. HANK enters.

HANK
You might need some help with that.

ANDY
I wouldn't mind. Who's going to help you with yours?

HANK
That damn plan to make this place a press station and bureau for a regional paper sat in our files for years. Then Airnet takes one look at it and decides it's best for business.

ANDY
Hank, you wrote that plan. You said we could make "more money printing other people's papers."

HANK
I did. It was a good business plan. I just didn't think they'd fire me and bring in one of their own guys to run it.

ANDY
How long have you been in this business?

HANK

Long enough to know, huh? At least they kept Matt on as a regional correspondent.

ANDY

I'm sure he'll get everything he deserves. What did they do with the furniture?

HANK

They moved it upstairs to the old advertising offices. I think they're going to rent this floor out and keep the nicer ones.

ANDY

And the nice furniture you just bought for yourself and the advertising department?

HANK

They took those to Arlington. *(HANK shrugs.)* It really was a good plan.

ANDY

I'm sure it was.

ANDY tapes up a box and nudges it to HANK

HANK

Golf injury, huh? *(ANDY nods.)* I didn't know you played.

ANDY

I don't. Probably part of my problem.

HANK picks up the box and starts to leave, but then stops.

HANK
Oh, I got a call from Bryant Williams? Said he won't be in today.

ANDY
Yeah, he got an offer with a publishing company. I sent him home to think about it.

HANK
Oh, so you knew? You got to another one, huh?

ANDY
Truth is, I think he got to me.

HANK
Nice to know I was right all along.

ANDY
Tell it to your next employer. You find anything yet?

HANK
No, but some friends in Lighthouse are looking for me. How about you?

ANDY
Not yet, but I have some things here I need to work out.

HANK
Sounds like you need a lawyer. Get a Philly this time, Zenger.

ANDY
I don't need one. We got a good judge instead. We're signing for an annulment.

HANK
That's good business. You'll save a lot. Congratulations.

ANDY
Forgive me if I don't celebrate.

HANK
I know. It's like this here. It's a shame really. This used to be an award-winning paper.

ANDY
Hank, they're all award-winning papers.

HANK
Yeah. But this one was ours.

- 30 -

www.ingramcontent.com/pod-product-compliance
Lightning Source LLC
Chambersburg PA
CBHW070959160426
43193CB00012B/1833